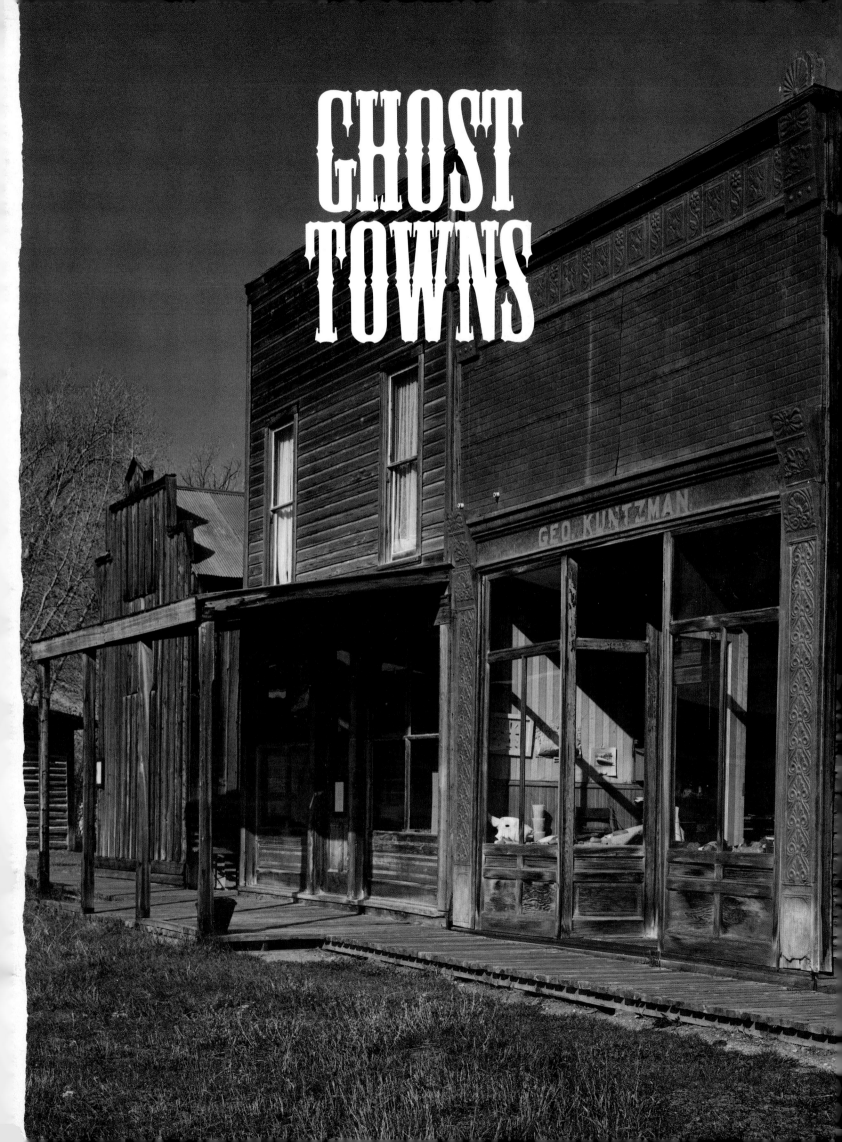
GHOST TOWNS

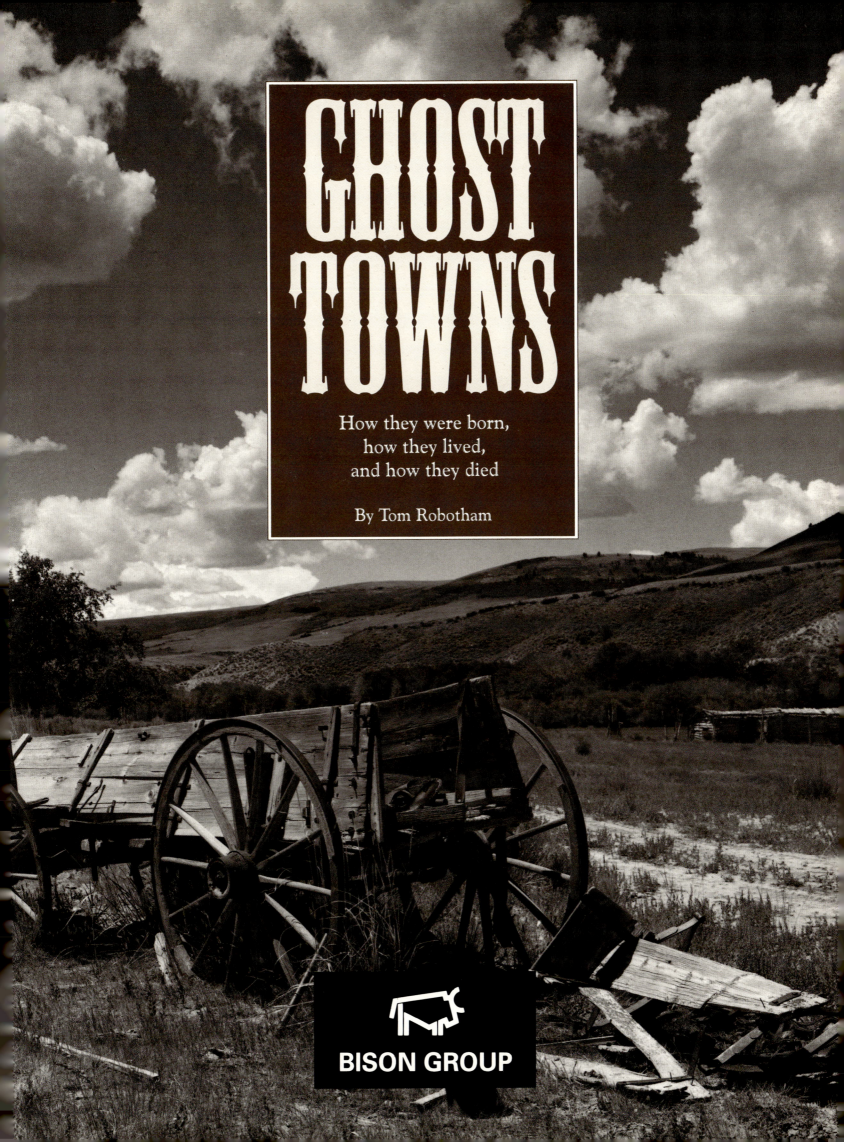

GHOST TOWNS

How they were born,
how they lived,
and how they died

By Tom Robotham

BISON GROUP

First published in 1993 by
Bison Books Ltd.
Kimbolton House
117A Fulham Road
London SW3 6RL

Copyright © 1993 Bison Books Ltd

All rights reserved. No part of this publication may be reproduced, stored in
a retrieval system or transmitted in any form by any means, electronic,
mechanical, photocopying or otherwise, without first obtaining the written
permissioin of the copyright owner.

ISBN 0 86124 963 1

Printed in Hong Kong

Page 1: A typical deserted copper-mining town in Wyoming. Such towns were
often abandoned not so much as a matter of survival but because prosperity
was not what it once had been.

Pages 2 and 3: Broken wagons, rusty farming tools, and a primitive log cabin,
mute symbols of the hardships faced by pioneers.

Below: Main street in Wasco, Oregon, a typical ghost town of the far West.

CONTENTS

Introduction	6
Prologue: The American Frontier	9
Gold! Gold From the American River!	13
California Boom Towns	21
The Forty-Niners	37
Farewell, Old California	51
Stark Mad For Silver	57
New Eldorados	69
Rustlers, Rascals, and Railroaders	89
Turn-of-the-Century Boom Towns	103
Epilogue: An Enduring Legacy	117
Index and Acknowledgments	127

INTRODUCTION

The ghost town is a powerful symbol of the American character. It reflects our transience, our readiness to move repeatedly in search of new opportunities. To be sure, transience is a feature of all cultures. Throughout history people have abandoned settlements because of fire, flood, enemy attack, or lack of basic resources, and such hardships have caused the decline of some American towns as well. But the classic American ghost town is less a product of the difficulties of *survival* than of the insatiable American pursuit of *prosperity*.

The American "clutches everything," observed Alexis de Toqueville in 1840, "but soon loosens his grasp to pursue fresh gratifications. . . . [He] builds a house in which to spend his old age, and sells it before the roof is on. . . ; he settles in a place, which he soon afterwards leaves to carry his changeable longings elsewhere."

This book is about places Americans have left behind. Not all the sites featured here are ghost towns in the conventional sense. Some survive in a kind of half-life as tourist attractions, while others have subsided into quiet little villages where landmarks from the boom years are preserved side by side with

Left: Main street in Aurora, Nevada, as it appeared in 1934. Aurora's fortunes rose and fell with the 1860s' silver rush.

Below: A fire engine house in Virginia City, Nevada. Fire was a major threat in 19th century boom towns in the West.

working businesses and well-kept residences. But many are truly ghostly, places where the visitor will find the skeletons of dusty, dilapidated buildings and nothing more. Finally, there are some places that have disappeared altogether, leaving only the outline of foundations to tell their stories. What all these abandoned and partially-abandoned communities have in common is that they were casualties of America's frontier mentality. Their inhabitants moved on because of the lure of greater prosperity to be found somewhere else. This was especially true of mining settlements – towns that sprang up all over the West during the gold and silver rushes that began in 1849.

By 1871, as Mark Twain noted in *Roughing It*, ghost towns ranged "far and wide over California." Gazing upon these towns, he wrote, "you will find it hard to believe that there stood at one time a fiercely flourishing little city, of two or three thousand souls, with its newspaper, fire company, brass band, volunteer militia, bank, hotels, noisy Fourth-of-July processions and speeches, gambling-hells crammed with tobacco smoke, profanity, and rough-bearded men of all nations and colors, with tables heaped with gold-dust sufficient for the revenues of a German principality. . . . and *now* nothing is left of it but a lifeless, homeless solitude." Even as Twain was writing this passage, other flourishing mining communities throughout the West were in fact ghost-towns-in-the-making.

It was not only the mining towns that went through boom-bust cycles. Some communities flourished as temporary terminals of railroad lines and declined rapidly when the terminus was moved. Others rose and fell during the great cattle drives of the 1870s and early 1880s. Still others suffered fates that defy generalization: one community in Kansas, for instance, became a ghost town when its residents moved to escape heavy debt.

A definitive survey of American ghost towns is impossible because many have disappeared without a trace, but even a comprehensive study of the ghost towns whose history has been preserved would be a mammoth undertaking. This book, therefore, is intended only as an introduction to a subject that has yet to be fully explored. Readers interested in pursuing the topic further would do well to look into the many excellent volumes that focus on ghost towns of individual states: Dan Fitzgerald's *Ghost Towns of Kansas* (Lawrence, KS: University Press of Kansas, 1988), is an especially interesting and informative example. To him, and to all the other historians of ghost towns, I extend my thanks.

Below: The residents of Georgetown, California, a little north of Sutter's Mill.

PROLOGUE: THE AMERICAN FRONTIER

By 1786, according to Thomas Jefferson, the inhabited parts of the United States contained an average of 10 people per square mile. "Wherever we reach [that density]," Jefferson wrote, "the inhabitants become uneasy, as too much compressed, and go off in great numbers to search for vacant country." Jefferson encouraged such movement as being good for the nation, as did other leaders. "This form of government," wrote James Madison in 1787, "in order to effect its purposes, must operate not within a small but an extensive sphere." And so, with the population approaching four million, the young nation began to expand across the Appalachian Mountains. After 1803, when Jefferson doubled American territory with the Louisiana Purchase, Americans began pushing back the frontier at an average rate of 17 miles per year.

One major reason for the migrations, as Jefferson noted, was simple availability of land for agriculture. Another, however, was the possibility of finding gold. In 1828 Benjamin Parks sparked America's first major gold rush when he discovered a nugget "as yellow as the yolk of an egg" in an area of Georgia then occupied only by Cherokee Indians. Soon thousands of miners had transformed the region.

Native Americans were not the only ones dismayed by this particular transformation. "I can hardly conceive of a more unmoral community that exists around these mines," wrote one newspaper correspondent. "Drunkenness, gambling, fighting, lewdness, and every other vice exist here to an awful extent. Many of the men, by working three days in the week, make several dollars, and then devote the remaining four to every species of vice."

The first town to spring up as a direct result of this gold rush was Auraria, which in its heyday included some two dozen stores, four or five taverns, a printing office, and approximately 1,000 inhabitants. But like so many boom towns that would follow, Auraria's fortunes soon declined when the gold played out and the miners abandoned it.

To be sure, not all Americans were as enthusiastic about westward expansion as Jefferson and Madison. "What do we want with this vast, worthless area, this region of savages and wild beasts," asked Daniel Webster, just eleven years before the California Gold Rush. "I will never vote one cent from the public treasury to place the Pacific Coast one inch nearer to Boston than it now is."

But most white Americans did not share Webster's sentiments, and, beginning in 1841, large numbers of wagon trains – filled with people who believed there was more to the West than savages and wild beasts – began to fan out across the Great Plains. The first transcontinental party during this phase of expansion gathered in the spring of 1841 in Independence, Missouri. Traveling in covered wagons, 69 men, women, and children – with $100 in cash among them – moved west for 1,000 miles, then split into two groups. One group made its way to California, while the other blazed what would become known

Below: A wagon train makes its way across a vast, desolate landscape. The westward migration began in earnest in 1841 after a small group of pioneers blazed the Oregon Trail.

as the Oregon Trail. In the next few years, thousands of others would follow in their footsteps.

One such pioneer was Francis Parkman, who departed from St. Louis in 1846. "Many of the emigrants," he wrote in *The Oregon Trail*, "especially those bound for California, were persons of wealth and standing. The hotels were crowded, and the gunsmiths and saddlers were kept constantly at work in providing arms and equipments for the different parties of travelers. Almost every day steamboats were leaving the levee and passing up the Missouri, crowded with passengers on their way to the frontier...."

The westward migration had undoubtedly been spurred by economic distress caused by the panic of 1837, but that was by no means its sole cause, for, as Parkman noted, many wealthy Americans seemed to feel compelled to move westward as well. The romance of adventurous travel across a virgin landscape, as well as a belief in America's Manifest Destiny, were, for some travelers, as motivating as the desire for personal prosperity. And the migration was further facilitated in the late 1840s when President James K. Polk acquired Oregon, through negotiation with the British, and California and New Mexico, as a result of the Mexican War.

Whatever material or spiritual benefits the Great Plains and Far West may have had to offer, the dangers of westward travel were still considerable. "The prairie is a strange place," wrote Parkman after several weeks on the trail. "A month ago I should have thought it rather a startling affair to have an acquaintance ride out in the morning and lose his scalp before night, but here it seems the most natural thing in the world."

In large part because of the dangers, there were still only about 15,000 people in California on the eve of the gold rush. San Francisco was still a little village, and white settlements were sparse throughout the rest of the state. Then someone discovered gold, and that seemed to outweigh all the dangers in the world. By 1852 California's population would be nearly a quarter of a million, and many a future ghost town would have begun its brief, gaudy existence.

Above: A painting by Benjamin Franklin Reinhart depicts a group of pioneers setting up camp for the evening.

Opposite top: An 1856 painting by Charles Wimar dramatically illustrates the dangers faced by pioneers as they crossed the Great Plains.

Right: A sign summarizes the history of Gold Canyon in Nevada.

Below: Francis Parkman, author of *The Oregon Trail*. Parkman's narrative is a classic, first-hand account of America's early westward migration.

PROLOGUE: THE AMERICAN FRONTIER

Above: The territorial expansion of the United States during the 19th century.

Below: San Francisco in 1851.

GOLD! GOLD FROM THE AMERICAN RIVER!

Among the earliest white settlers in California was John Augustus Sutter, a German-born Swiss who had come to North America in 1834 to avoid debtor's prison. After living in St. Louis for several years, Sutter set out for the Pacific Northwest in the company of some fur traders, then took a ship to Hawaii. Finally, in 1839, he settled in California, which was at the time still Mexican territory.

In 1840 "Captain Sutter," as he now styled himself, became a Mexican citizen, and a year later he convinced the Mexican governor of the territory to grant him 50,000 acres so he could build a farming and ranching community that would serve the surrounding area. The grant lay in a fertile valley east of San Francisco, and it was here, at the confluence of the Sacramento and American rivers, that Sutter built his headquarters – a fort and stockade – which he called New Helvetia.

Within a few years Sutter was operating a trading post and several flour mills, as well as farms and ranches. Ever-anxious to expand and diversify, he realized he would soon need a good source of finished lumber and decided to build his own sawmill to fill this need. It was a decision that would ultimately result in his own downfall while dramatically altering the landscape and the lives of countless Americans.

In the spring of 1847 Sutter hired a carpenter named James W. Marshall to supervise construction of the mill. Marshall set out in May to search for a suitable site and soon found one on the

Below Left: A portrait of John Augustus Sutter by Samuel S. Osgood.

Below: James M. Marshall, who changed the course of American history with his accidental discovery of gold at Sutter's Mill in 1848.

south fork of the American River, about 50 miles from the fort. Construction began in August. "Our first business was to put up log houses, as we intended to remain here all winter," Marshall wrote later. "This was done in less than no time, for my men were great with an axe." Work proceeded into the new year.

Above: Marshall's cabin at Sutter's Mill.

Right: The site of Marshall's discovery. "I shall never forget that morning," Marshall recalled years later. "[My] eye caught a glimpse of something shining at the bottom of the ditch. . . . I reached my hand down and picked it up; it made my heart thump for I felt certain it was gold."

One morning in January, Marshall went for a walk to inspect the mill race. "I shall never forget that morning," he recalled. "As I was taking my usual walk along the race, after shutting off the water, my eye caught a glimpse of something shining at the bottom of the ditch. There was about a foot of water running down there. I reached my hand down and picked it up; it made my heart thump for I felt certain it was gold."

Upon returning to his cabin for breakfast, Marshall showed the nuggets to his men and told them he thought he had found gold. Some thought he was crazy, he later recalled, but others were excited. After that, he said, "we always kept a sharp lookout, and in the course of three or four days we had picked up about three ounces – our work [on the mill] still progressing as lively as ever, for none of us imagined at that time that the whole country was sowed with gold."

About a week after the initial discovery Marshall decided to travel back to Sutter's Fort to inform his boss. When he arrived, Marshall told Sutter he had important news and insisted that they speak in private. Once the men were safely behind locked doors, Marshall unfolded a handkerchief and revealed the gold nuggets. Sutter "at once declared it was gold," Marshall wrote, but he was less sure about the nuggets' purity. After consulting an encyclopedia, the two men tested the weight and density of the nuggets and determined that they were "entirely pure."

"This fact being ascertained," Marshall wrote, "we thought it our best policy to keep it as quiet as possible till we . . . finished our mill. . . ." It proved to be an ineffective precaution. "Soon," according to Marshall, "the whole country was in a bustle. I had scarcely arrived at the mill again [before] several persons appeared with pans, shovels and hoes, and those that had not iron picks had wooden ones, all anxious to fall to work and dig up our mill."

Sutter knew he had no official claim to the land on which he had constructed his mill. Once gold was discovered, he attemptd to secure the land by negotiating a lease with the Indians who had previously occupied it. But he was aware that this lease would not carry much weight in the long run, so he drafted a letter asking the military governor of the territory to endorse the lease. He assigned one of his workers, Charles Bennett, to carry the letter, along with several gold nuggets as proof

Below: Four of James Marshall's contemporaries and fellow miners.

Above: An advertisement notifying Parisians of an expedition to California gold country. By the end of 1849 would-be miners from around the world were pouring into the region.

Right: A woodcut depicts James Marshall performing one of several tests on his nuggets to determine whether it was, in fact, gold.

of his find. Although Sutter had sworn him to secrecy, Bennett could not contain himself. All along the way he boasted that the find would "make this the greatest country in the world."

Word spread farther when, on March 15, a San Francisco newspaper published a report of the strike. Even so, the gold strike remained largely a local phenomenon until May, when a man named Sam Brannan entered the picture.

Brannan, a Mormon elder, had led more than two hundred followers to Yerba Buena (the original name for San Francisco), via Cape Horn, while the United States was at war with Mexico. He subsequently traveled to Utah, where he tried to persuade Brigham Young that California was the perfect spot for a Mormon community, but Young declined, feeling that the Utah location he had found was superior.

On his way back to California, Brannan stopped in Sutter's Fort and decided to stay awhile. Sensing a business opportunity amidst the bustle of Sutter's pre-gold-rush empire, Brannan opened a store. When a young man named Jacob Wittmer, a teamster working for Marshall, entered the store one day and offered a bottle of gold dust in exchange for a bottle of liquor, the course of history was changed forever.

Traveling back to San Francisco, Brannan could scarcely contain himself. "Gold! Gold! Gold from the American River!" he shouted as he walked the streets of the budding city while waving the bottle of gold dust high over his head. The sight of gold in the hands of one of their neighbors proved far more compelling to San Franciscans than any newspaper accounts, and soon the city was buzzing with excitement. Brannan, meanwhile, returned to his store near Sutter's Mill and quickly stocked it with picks, shovels, and other equipment to serve the men he had stirred up.

By mid-June nearly 75 percent of the men in San Francisco had left town to seek gold. Signs reading "Gone to the Diggings" appeared in many a store window, while those merchants who stayed behind also adapted themselves to the new times. The price of a shovel jumped from one dollar to ten, and other items were similarly priced to meet demand. By July men from southern California and even Hawaii were rushing to the mines, and by the end of the year men from as far away as Chile, Australia, and China were pouring into the region.

On December 5 President Polk told Congress that more than 4,000 men were actively engaged in the search for gold. The accounts of abundance, he said, "would scarcely command belief, were they not corroborated. . . ." The next day, taking their cue from the President, a shipload of would-be miners set sail from Boston to San Francisco, via Cape Horn. It was a 13,000 mile voyage, but the promise of riches again suppressed concern over hardship. Within the next 12 months hundreds of ships took the same trip, while countless wagon trains set out on the grueling 5-month overland journey to the promised land of gold-country. The day of the gold rush boom towns was now at hand.

Above: Prospectors share a meal during their journey to gold country.

Overleaf: A poster advertises passage to California from New Bedford, Mass. The voyage from the Northeast to California was some 13,000 miles via Cape Horn. It was a grueling journey. But for thousands of Forty-Niners dreams of riches made the hardships tolerable.

FOR CALIFORNIA
AND THE
GOLD REGION DIRECT!

The Magnificent, Fast Sailing and favorite packet Ship,

JOSEPHINE,
BURTHEN 400 TONS, CAPT.

Built in the most *superb* manner of Live Oak, White Oak and Locust, for a New York and Liverpool Packet; thoroughly Copper-fastened and Coppered. She is a very fast sailer, having crossed the Atlantic from Liverpool to New-York in 14 days, the shortest passage ever made by a *Sailing Ship*. Has superior accommodations for Passengers, can take Gentlemen with their Ladies and families. Will probably reach SAN FRANCISCO **THIRTY DAYS** ahead of any Ship sailing at the same time. Will sail about the

10th November Next.

For Freight or Passage apply to the subscriber,

RODNEY FRENCH,
New Bedford, October 15th.   No. 103 North Water Street, Rodman's Wharf.

CALIFORNIA BOOM TOWNS

Ships that set sail for the gold rush ended their voyage in San Francisco, and the city was dramatically transformed as a result. Although many of its 3,000 residents had departed for the diggings in 1848, new arrivals soon filled the void, and by the end of 1849 San Francisco's population had jumped to 20,000. It was, however, a population constantly in flux. Newcomers might stay for a few weeks, perhaps making money by selling some of their possessions at exorbitant prices, and then move on to the diggings. "Veteran" miners, meanwhile, would visit the city to deposit their new-found riches in a bank, send it back home, or spend it on liquor, whores, and gambling.

The real action, of course, was not in San Francisco but in the hundreds of mining settlements that were springing up all across the western slopes of the Sierra Nevada Mountains. The gold miners were concentrated in what came to be known as the Mother Lode country – a 120-mile strip of gold-rich land in the Sierra Nevada foothills. (This region today straddles Highway 49 and spans nine counties: Madera, Mariposa, Tuolumne, Calaveras, Amador, El Dorado, Placer, Nevada, and Sierra.) Some of the settlements in the region would never be more than camps, but others quickly became full-blown towns. And while such boom towns might differ in their particulars, all were fundamentally alike both in their character and in the way they came into being. In 1855 a writer named Louise Clappe described what typically happened: "Sometimes a company of . . . [miners] will find itself upon a bar where a few pieces of the precious metal lie scattered upon the surface of the ground. Of course they immediately prospect it, which is accomplished by panning out a few basinfuls of soil. If it pays, they claim the spot and build their shanties. The news spreads that wonderful diggings have been discovered. . . . The monte-leaders – those worse than fiends – rush, vulture like, upon the scene and erect a round tent, where, in gambling, drinking, swearing, and fighting, the many reproduce pandemonium in more than its original horror, while a few honestly and industriously commence digging for gold, and lo! as if a fairy's wand had been waved above the bar, a full-grown mining town hath sprung into existence."

Some of these towns would rapidly decline when rumors of better prospects elsewhere began to circulate. Others, however, survived the ups and downs of the mining boom because of their location along heavily traveled routes. Thus it is that today the better-known surviving California mining towns are almost always surrounded by clusters of smaller ghost towns and ghost camps.

The first town to emerge from the gold rush – the town that sprang up around Sutter's Mill – was Coloma. Charles B. Gillespie, a miner working near Coloma in its heyday, recalled a typical Sunday afternoon in the town. The main street, he said, "was alive with crowds" of "ragged, dirty" men who were nonetheless "goodnatured." Street hustlers, inducing miners to try their hands at various games of chance, could be found on every corner, while in a nearby house Gillespie took in a sermon, which ended with a telling statement by the preacher: "There will be a divine service in this house next Sabbath – if in the meantime I hear of no new diggings."

Word of new diggings came quickly enough, and Coloma eventually lost the boisterous crowds described by Gillespie. It never died completely, however, for today it is owned largely by the state and is preserved as an historic park.

Another town established early on was Placerville, just south of Coloma. In the summer of 1848 three men discovered gold there and named it Dry Diggings because the stream in which they were panning was very shallow. Over the next three years locals changed the name to Old Dry Diggings, Ravine City, and then Hangtown (the last when the town became the site of the first lynching in gold rush country). By 1851 Hangtown had finally become known as Placerville. That year, a Scottish artist named J.D. Borthwick arrived and recorded his observations. The town was, he wrote, "one long straggling street of clapboard houses and log cabins, built in a hollow at the side of a creek, and surrounded by high and steep hills. . . . Along the

Below: An advertisement for mining supplies. The ad's claim notwithstanding, prices for supplies were usually exorbitant due to the overwhelming demand. In the summer of 1848, for instance, the price of a shovel in San Francisco jumped from one dollar to ten.

148. Mormon Island Emporium, Excelsior Tent

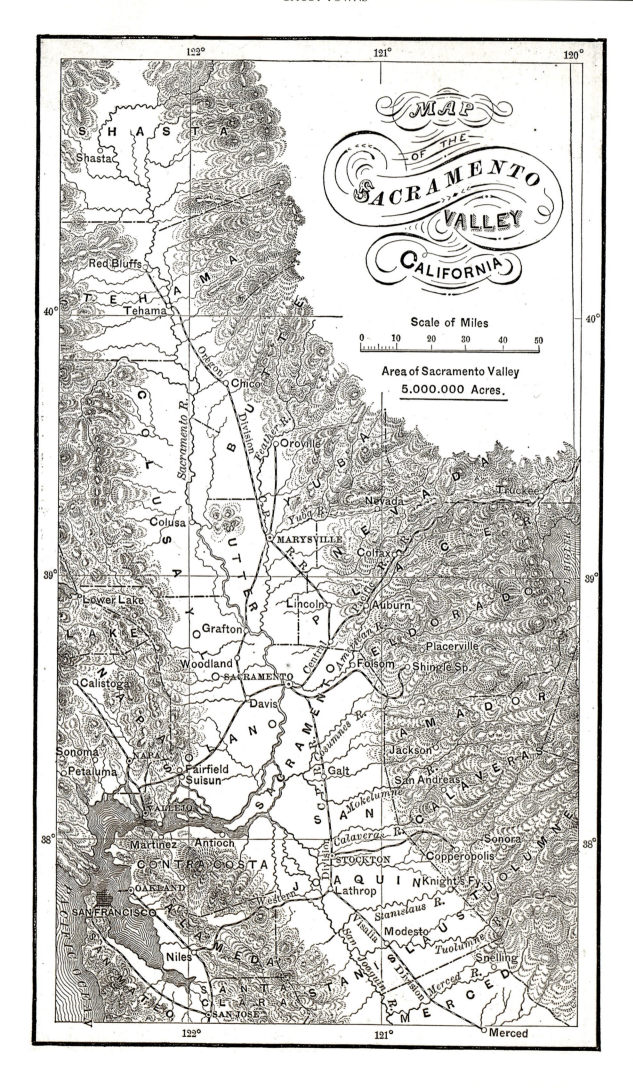

CALIFORNIA BOOM TOWNS

Left: A map of California gold country, also known as the Mother Lode. The region spans nine counties and today straddles Highway 49.

Above: Forty-Niners pan for gold in a Californian stream. When such efforts were successful, word spread quickly, transforming tent camps into full-blown towns in a matter of weeks.

Below: A view of the American River, near Coloma, California, the first town to emerge as a result of the Gold Rush.

23

Left: A church in Coloma, California. While many boom towns had churches, religion was not a top priority for most miners.

Above: A stone marker at the site where James Marshall made his discovery.

whole length of the creek, as far as one could see, on the banks of the creek, in the ravines, in the middle of the . . . street . . . and even inside some of the houses were parties of miners, numbering from three or four to a dozen, all hard at work. . . . There was continual noise and clatter, as mud, dirt, stones, and water were thrown about in all directions; and the men, dressed in ragged clothes and big boots, wielding picks and shovels . . . were all working as if for their lives. . . . "

That Placerville continued to thrive after the gold rush is probably due solely to the fact of its location along the Overland Trail. Today it is located along Highway 50, one of the main routes to Lake Tahoe.

Unlike Placerville, the town of Volcano would tumble into obscurity after the mining boom, though, historically, it was among the most important of the mining towns. Local legend has it that gold was discovered in Volcano even before it was discovered at Sutter's Mill. This claim has never been proven and continues to be a point of debate, but it is certainly true that it didn't take long for gold-seekers to discover the place after the rush began. Fortunate miners reported panning anywhere from $100 to $1,000 of gold a day there, with some dredging up $500 in a single pan. By the end of the decade some $90,000,000-worth of bullion had been shipped from Volcano.

When word of these strikes spread, the town expanded quickly. Soon it had a population of more than 8,000 people, who were served by nearly 50 saloons, two breweries, five hotels, numerous restaurants, a church, a theater company, a library, and a jail. To accommodate the many shipments of gold to San Francisco banks, branches of Wells Fargo and Adams Express were also established in Volcano. And because of its wealth, the town also had more than its share of bandits: indeed, bandits held up their stage coaches so often that both the Wells Fargo and Adams Express offices were eventually forced to close down.

Below: Placerville, just south of Coloma, California. In 1849, Placerville – then called Dry Diggings – was the site of the first lynching in the region. Shortly thereafter, it was re-named Hangtown. The residents changed the name to Placerville in 1851.

Previous pages: A saloon in Placerville. Drinking establishments were considered essential to any boom town.

Above: A view of Placerville in 1900. Placerville continued to thrive long after the Gold Rush because of its location along the Overland Trail.

Right: Miners pan for gold along the Mokelumne River. The town of Mokelumne Hill was one of the earliest gold-rush communities.

Like Coloma, Volcano never died completely, and in recent years it has been maintained by a sparse population and by a regular stream of tourists who come to see the old Wells Fargo building, the magnificent St. George Hotel, and other relics of the gold-rush years.

Another of the earliest Gold Rush towns was Mokelumne Hill. The town got off to a rocky start when miners there found themselves short of food and supplies. Within a year, however, some of the more enterprising settlers had set up stores, and "Moke Hill," as it was usually called, became a thriving tent camp. Gradually wooden structures replaced the tents, and later, after a devastating fire, stone buildings became the norm.

While the town was growing it was one of the most violent in the state, in large part because of bitter clashes between gangs of Chilean and American prospectors. Eventually, however, Moke Hill became more civilized, and at one point it even boasted a rather lavish theater. Today the town is the site of several interesting structures left over from gold rush days, including remains of a store and a hotel.

The gold in Angels Camp was reportedly discovered by accident one day while a man named Bennager Rasberry was out hunting jackrabbits. According to the story, the ramrod of Rasberry's rifle got stuck in the barrel. Unable to pull it out, he fired the gun, propelling the ramrod into a nearby rock. When he went to retrieve what was left of the ramrod he discovered that it had broken loose a piece of gold ore. Before long, Rasberry was a rich man – and the founder of a new town.

Among the men who poured into the area upon hearing of Rasberry's strike was George Angel. Perhaps more sensible than most miners, Angel realized the chances of becoming rich at mining were small. He tried his luck in the diggings, to be sure, but to hedge his bets he also established the first businesses in the area, a trading post and beer hall.

Although Angels Camp was not atypical in most respects, its reputation was spread far afield by two of its visitors: Bret Harte and Mark Twain. The town, in fact, provided the setting for one of Harte's most famous stories, "Luck of Roaring Camp," and it was here also that Twain gathered material for his story "The Celebrated Jumping Frog of Calaveras County."

Angels Camp flourished longer than most gold rush towns, with mining in the area continuing almost to the close of the century. In this century, it has survived in large part as a tourist attraction and is, in the eyes of many, one of the most endearing towns of the entire Mother Lode region. (The Calaveras County Fair still features frog jumping contests in recognition of one of the tales that made the town famous.)

Sonora, another town with a colorful history, was initially a

Below: The old hoisting plant at Angels Mine in Calaveras County. Mark Twain and Bret Harte were among those who visited the town in its heyday.

Mexican settlement that was destined to be taken over by miners. "I had never seen a more beautiful, a more romantic spot, than Sonora," recalled William Perkins, a Canadian who arrived in 1849. "On Saturdays and Sundays, the camp used to wear, night and day, an almost magic appearance. Lights shone from gaily decorated houses, all of them with their fronts open to the streets, and the streets themselves strewn with lighted tapers!"

The romantic aura quickly faded, however, after a party of Philadelphians founded the nearby town of Woods Crossing. As the new community boomed, Sonora's fortunes declined, and it gained a reputation for violence and seediness. By the end of the century it was all but abandoned by miners, but the town has nevertheless somehow managed to survive into our own time. Today Sonora's numerous adobe structures reflect the town's Mexican heritage, while the Victorian homes in the area are relics of the Anglo-American influence that came later. Perhaps the most historic building in the town, however, is what is today the Tuolumne County Museum: built in 1857, it was originally the town's jailhouse.

Just a few miles from Sonora another town emerged. It, too, had been a Mexican settlement, but it changed hands in March 1850 after a party led by Thaddeus Hildreth set up camp there. Within a few days of their arrival, Hildreth and his men had unearthed 30 pounds of gold. They quickly chased away the local Mexicans, but soon other miners began pouring in from Sonora and other nearby towns and camps. Within a month 5,000 men had come to Hildreth's Diggings, and by 1851 the town (now called Columbia) boasted its own newspaper, three theatres, two fire companies, several banks, three churches, and eight hotels, in addition to the usual array of saloons, livery stables, warehouses, and general stores.

Although no accurate population records exist for Columbia, it is estimated that the town had between 15,000 and 30,000 residents by 1853, though as was the case in most mining towns, Columbia's population was extremely transient. Huge fires in

Above: A waterwheel at Angels Camp.

Right: Bret Harte. Angels Camp provided the setting for Harte's story "The Luck of Roaring Camp."

Opposite: A saloon at Angels Camp.

1854 and 1857 heightened this instability, and after the second fire, the population dropped back to about 5,000. By the early 1860s much of the town had been abandoned, though some mines remained active there until about 1880. Today, Columbia is preserved as a state historic park, and the town has been painstakingly restored.

The origins of Chinese Camp, located about 25 miles south of Sonora, are unclear. According to one legend, a group of Englishmen in 1849 brought in a large number of Chinese to help work their claims. Another legend has it that a ship's captain abandoned his vessel in San Francisco bay in the early days of the gold rush and brought his entire Chinese crew to gold country. In any event, the settlement eventually was home to some 5,000 Chinese, though it contained many other nationalities as well. There were, for instance, enough Americans and Mexicans to build a Catholic Church, a Masonic Temple, and a Sons of Temperance Lodge. Today Chinese Camp, close to the junction of Highways 49 and 120, is all but deserted.

Right: John C. Frémont, one of America's most famous explorers and army officers. In 1849 Frémont established a settlement near the southern tip of the Mother Lode region. The town of Mariposa later grew up around it.

Above: The Mariposa Gazette office in California. Although many of the town's structures have disappeared, a few important buildings remain.

Not far from the southern tip of the Mother Lode region lies the town of Mariposa (the Spanish word for "butterfly"). John C. Frémont, one of America's great explorers, first established a settlement there in the summer of 1849. The area had not been Frémont's first choice for the site of the ranch he wanted to build, but any disappointment he may have felt was probably not permanent: within two years his ranch had become the locus of the richest strike in the entire state.

As miners poured into the region, illegal claims became a constant problem, and by the mid-1850s, Frémont found himself mired in disputes. The biggest dispute came when the Merced Mining Company "jumped" two of Frémont's claims. Initially, Frémont had filed a lawsuit instead of attempting to drive the claim-jumpers off himself, but by the summer of 1858 he had decided that a more direct form of action was called for. Thus, when more than 50 men attempted to jump a third claim that July, Frémont was ready for them, having stationed armed

guards at the site. The claim jumpers settled in for a siege, and refused to surrender even when the sheriff arrived. Only after the governor sent a messenger warning that the militia would be sent in if necessary did the Merced men disperse.

By 1861 Frémont was facing new troubles – this time of a financial nature – and he eventually lost his ranch, the land being subsequently divided up and sold. But though Frémont's Mariposa ranch did not survive, the town that grew up near it did. Today it is the site of several important historic buildings, including a courthouse built in 1854. (It is still in use today.) The nearby Mariposa County Museum and History Center contains an exceptional gold rush exhibit, which includes a number of items that belonged to Frémont.

Although most of California's gold-rush activity took place south of Sutter's Mill, other miners had success north of the original discovery. Among the northern-most towns in the region is Downieville, established in 1849 after William Downie, a Scotsman, and 13 other men struck gold there. Within a short time other miners poured into the region, and Downieville's population ultimately reached 5,000. Before the decade ended, however, the gold was beginning to thin out, and most of the miners left. To make matters worse, the town was devastated by fire in 1858. Yet a few residents did come back to rebuild, and the town has lingered on to this day. A courthouse built in 1855 still stands, as does an old gallows.

Located a little to the southwest of Downieville is the town of Rough and Ready, so named because its founders had served under General Zachary "Old Rough and Ready" Taylor. For a time the town had only one community building, an 18- by-36-

Left: In addition to a telegraph office, like the one pictured here, the bigger boom towns boasted several banks, a variety of hotels, a newspaper, theaters, and, of course, numerous saloons.

Below: Mariposa in the mid-19th century. The photographer, Charles Bierstadt, was the brother of landscape painter Albert Bierstadt.

33

foot log cabin that served as both the courthouse and the saloon. Legend has it that the judge would rarely attempt to stop the card games and drinking while he was conducting a trial but instead would simply tell the gamblers to "call their games low."

Other towns were similarly casual when it came to the law, but whereas most of them became more formal as they grew, Rough and Ready remained fiercely independent. When word came that the town would be subject to federal taxes, the citizens of Rough and Ready passed a resolution to "withdraw from the territory of California and from the United States of America to form . . . the Great Republic of Rough and Ready."

The resolution stipulated that the withdrawal would be peaceful if possible, but violent if necessary. The miners then went on to elect E.F. Brundage president of the new "republic" and even to draw up a constitution. Amused territorial and federal officials simply ignored all this, and the miners eventually gave up.

In spite of a devastating fire, Rough and Ready flourished until about 1870, when its mines became depleted. Yet it has contrived to survive into this century and is today the site of a collection of rather interesting old buildings which have the added charm of reminding visitors of one of the most absurd secession attempts in U.S. history.

CALIFORNIA BOOM TOWNS

Left: The Mariposa County courthouse, which is still in use today.

Above: Miners gather on the main street of Downieville, located near the northern end of gold country. At its peak, the town had a population of 5,000.

Below: The town of Rough and Ready, named after Zachary Taylor. In 1859, after learning that they were to be subjected to new federal taxes, residents of the town decided to secede from the Union and form an independent Republic. Federal officials simply ignored the announcement, and the miners eventually gave up their fight for freedom.

THE FORTY-NINERS

The men who came to California during the gold rush were, according to Mark Twain, "a driving, vigorous" bunch, "an assemblage of two hundred thousand *young* men – not simpering, dainty, kid-gloved weaklings, but stalwart, muscular, dauntless young braves, brimful of push and energy, and royally endowed with every attribute that goes to make a peerless and magnificent manhood – the very pick and choice of the world's glorious ones. . . ."

Left: A Forty-Niner poses with his equipment and a hefty sack of gold. The men who came to the gold rush, according to Mark Twain, were "a driving vigorous bunch . . . the very pick and choice of the world's glorious ones." In reality, the miners came from all walks of life, including the dregs of society.

Below: A miner takes a break outside his cabin. Many early prospectors were lucky to have shelters even this primitive.

As the ghost-town historian Robert Silverberg has noted, this description may be a bit too romantic. Far from being "the world's glorious ones," many of the men who descended on California in those days were filthy, violent, and without moral restraint. Others, to be sure, were upstanding men simply trying to make money for families back home, but the forty-niners were at best a mixed group: more adventurous than many Americans, perhaps, but certainly no more gifted or virtuous, good men to found new towns, but not necessarily the best men to make them work. The sheer variety of backgrounds represented is one of the most striking aspects of the gold rush. In San Francisco, enclaves called Little Chile, Little Germany, Little France, Chinatown, and Sydney Town (for British convicts who had come from exile in Australia) arose quickly; and all these groups, as well as blacks from the South, were represented in the mining camps.

In light of the unprecedented mix of groups working so closely together, it is surprising that there was relatively little crime in the region during the first year of the gold rush. Some historians have suggested that the lack of crime during this early phase was due to the plethora of gold: finding it was easier than stealing someone else's. It may also be that at first there was a spirit of comraderie, as there often is when strangers are thrown together in unfamiliar conditions. In any event, it was not until 1849 that robbery and other crimes became a problem. And since there were no established courts or law enforcement agencies to deal with crime, the miners perforce took matters into their own hands and resorted to vigilantism.

The region's first lynching occurred in January 1849 in a town called Dry Diggings. The trouble started when five bandits entered a Mexican gambler's hotel room, held a pistol to his head, and demanded his money. Ignoring the threat to his life, the gambler yelled for help, and before the robbers could react, neighboring miners rushed in to capture them. After subduing the bandits, the miners selected a temporary judge and jury and,

Previous pages: Miners gather at the Omaha Mine in Nevada County, California.

Right: A lynching in gold-rush country. The first lynching of the gold rush occurred in January 1849, after five bandits were apprehended attempting to rob a Mexican gambler in his hotel room in Placerville, California. The accused were given no time for explanation. One witness said the mob "would listen to nothing contrary to their brutal desires."

Below: A Chinese store in Coulterville. Chinese were often victims of violence at the hands of white miners.

Above: An abandoned Mexican meeting place in Hornitos. Like the Chinese, the Mexicans were often the victims of violence and discrimination.

Below: Another of the remaining structures in Hornitos, which was the site of an unusually brutal lynching of a Chinese miner.

in short order, sentenced the five men to 39 lashes (a traditional punishment which, in this country dates back to colonial times and is actually rooted in the Bible.) Three of the men – two Frenchmen and a Chilean – were then accused of a murder-robbery that had occurred several months earlier in a nearby camp. The mob-jury at once decided that the men must be guilty and should be hanged.

"No time was given them for explanation," wrote E. Gould Buffum, a witness. Buffum added that he protested on their behalf, but to no avail. The crowd, "excited by frequent and deep potations of liquor, would listen to nothing contrary to their brutal desires, and even threatened to hang me if I did not immediately desist from further remarks. "[T]he accused vainly tried to speak, but none of them understanding English, they were obliged to employ their native tongues, which few of those assembled understood. Vainly they called for an an interpreter, for their cries were drowned out by the yells of the now infuriated mob." A short time later all three men were hanged "without priest or prayer book." For the next two years the community was known as Hangtown. (Eventually, the name was changed to Placerville. See Chapter 2).

Lynchings were not uncommon during the gold rush, and, in spite of the cavalier nature of the proceedings, most contemporary observers agreed that such vigilantism was necessary. As a *New York Times* editorial noted in 1851, the laws in California were "inefficient . . . and the means of confinement of offenders so insecure that the chances were in favor of their escape." But not all lynchings met with the same degree of approval. On July 4, 1881, in the town of Downieville, a Mexican woman stabbed a white miner named Jack Cannon while Cannon was harassing her. The woman tried to flee was but was quickly caught and dragged to the center of town. Again an impromptu "trial" was conducted, and the woman was found guilty. She was subsequently hanged from a nearby bridge. When word of this lynching spread to other towns, people were horrified. Much as they might sympathize with the need for vigilantism in general, most miners could not countenance the thought of lynching a woman.

Some exceedingly disreputable lynchings, on the other hand, went virtually unnoticed. In Hornitos, one of a number of mining towns with large Chinese populations, a lynching resulted from the pervasive tension between Chinese and whites. Trouble started one day when a group of white boys began tormenting a Chinese miner named Charley. According to one account, Charley fired his gun to scare the boys off but accidentally hit one of them in the leg. Charley was quickly apprehended and thrown in jail. That night a group of men gathered outside his cell and began talking to him in a friendly manner, saying they realized the shooting was an accident and that Charley would be released the next day. One of them even offered Charley a pipeful of tobacco. When Charley reached for it, however, the men threw a noose around his neck and began slamming his head against the cell wall. Charley died, but the entire mob went unpunished.

Not all the violence against Chinese miners came from whites. Various Chinese tongs (secret societies) seem to have been quite as capable of anti-Chinese violence as any whites. In 1856, for instance, two tongs clashed at Chinese Camp, the largest Chinese community in the Mother Lode region, and when the fighting ended four men were dead and four more were seriously wounded.

The most consistently violent men in the region were, of course, the professional outlaws. Among the most notorious was Joaquin Murieta, who terrorized Calaveras county during

NOTORIOUS CALIFORNIA OUTLAW

Left: Miners brave the cold while waiting in line to record their claim. Each community established its own regulations regarding claims. In spite of such regulations, claim-jumping was common.

Above: Miners confront each other in a saloon. Brawls and gunfights were common in boom towns.

Left, top: A painting of Joaquin Murieta, a legendary Mexican bandit who terrorized Calaveras county during much of 1853.

Left, bottom: An anti-Chinese riot. Not all violence against Chinese miners came from whites. Various Chinese tongs (secret societies) attacked each other in clashes over mining rights.

much of 1853. Murieta first came to the attention of the miners in the region in January 1853. Suspected of stealing horses, the Mexican bandit was captured but soon escaped with the help of his gang. Rather than go into hiding, Murieta and his men then proceeded to crisscross the region, killing white miners on sight. Rising up in anger at these killings, the whites of Calaveras county proceeded to lynch three Mexicans, although they had no evidence that these men were members of Murieta's gang, and the Calaveras men then ordered all other Mexicans out of the county. For the next several months this pattern of random violence and hasty retribution continued.

Finally, on May 25, a group of whites clashed with a group of Mexican outlaws, the leader of the Mexican gang was killed, and the white vigilantes subsequently concluded it was Murieta. To prove it, they cut off his head, preserved it in a container of alcohol, and put it on public display. (To this day we have no idea whether the head was actually that of Joaquin Murieta.)

If the miners who erected the gold rush boom towns had difficulty in dealing with the problem of violent crime, they had trouble with the more mundane aspects of maintaining law and order as well – even to the relatively simple matter of regulating mining operations. Since there were initially no state laws governing the mining operations, each mining community created its own set of regulations to determine the process of staking claims, the standard dimension for each, rules for holding and forfeiting claims, and so on. But as more whites poured into the region, intolerance toward foreigners increased, and some towns passed laws designed to put foreign miners at a disadvantage. The state legislature, for instance, passed a Foreign Miners' Tax Law in 1850, which imposed a monthly fee of $20 on all miners of foreign birth (enforced most vigilantly against Chinese and Mexicans.) Some foreigners paid the tax, others did not. The Mexicans in Sonora refused to pay the tax and assigned armed guards to ward them off the collectors. Tension increased, and at one point several Mexicans were nearly lynched, having supposedly committed a murder. Cooler heads prevailed, and the lynching was prevented, but most Mexicans eventually abandoned the town as a result of the incident.

Another potential source of trouble was gambling, which, next to mining and drinking, was perhaps the most common activity for miners. It was naturally not uncommon for fights to erupt in the midst of a poker game whenever one player suspected another of cheating. A visitor to Hornitos in 1857 reported that he was passing some gambling tables when two players drew knives on each other. The dealer was one step ahead of them, however: drawing his pistol, he ordered the troublemakers to leave the table, and the gaming was then resumed as though nothing untoward had happened.

Although card games were the most popular form of gambling, the more cultivated gamblers might also be found playing chess, backgammon, and billiards. Other forms of recreation (which naturally involved betting) included bull-bear fights, wrestling, and boxing. In addition, towns that had theaters brought in traveling drama groups and minstrel shows. The mere presence of a theater did not, however, mean a town was especially sophisticated, for theater audiences could be as raucous as any saloon crowd. Performers who did not immediately win over audiences were often pelted with garbage or harried in

Below: Miners pass the time playing cards. Although card games were the most popular form of gambling, backgammon, billiards, and other games were also common, at least in the larger towns.

THE FORTY-NINERS

Above: Saloons were the only social centers in many towns. To compete, the wealthier saloon-keepers often served free lunches.

Below: The dining room of the luxurious Hotel de Paris in Georgetown County, Colorado. In addition to fine hotels, many boom towns also boasted elaborate theaters – none of which had much to do with the miners' actual state of refinement.

other ways. One night in Mokelumne Hill, for example, a young actor was performing Richard III, unaware that a burro had been smuggled into the theater and was about to steal the show. When the actor shouted out the play's most famous line, "My kingdom for a horse," the burro began braying loudly, undoubtedly at the urging of the practical jokers. The delighted audience howled with laughter while the actor dashed from the theater in shame.

In all gold rush boom towns the center of social life was the saloon. The better establishments were elaborately decorated and served free lunches, while saloons in more dangerous towns provided their customers with another service: bags of sand which could be used for cover in the event of a gunfight.

Pioneer preachers made meager attempts to bring some sense of moral restraint into the California mining towns, but by and large religion was not a major force among the forty-niners. While most Christian denominations were represented, and while many towns had churches, the miners were generally too distracted to be good church-goers. Preachers, too, left their congregations to try their luck at the diggings.

The state of public health in the boom towns also left a good deal to be desired. The typical diet included bread, jerked beef, and sometimes beans and rice. Vegetables were rare, and this deficiency often resulted in scurvy. Impure water, meanwhile, made cholera an even greater health problem, just as it had been during the journey west.

Housing was generally inadequate, especially in the early days. Often, the first men to arrive in a camp would be without even wagons or tents in which to sleep and had to dig caves for shelter. Houses were built once a camp showed signs of permanence, but until the late 1850s these tended to be merely light

Above: The Old Mission Church, near Cataldo, Idaho. Mining areas did not usually lack churches, but preachers were not above leaving their congregations if they learned of a new gold strike.

Below: Miners eating dinner in their cabin. The typical diet consisted of bread and jerked beef. The absence of vegetables made scurvy a common problem.

THE FORTY-NINERS

Above and below: Housing was often inadequate in boom towns. Many miners lacked even wagons or tents and had to dig caves for shelter. Wooden structures, like the ones pictured here, were highly vulnerable to fire, but most miners could not afford to build homes out of stone or brick.

PLACER MINING, HUMBOLDT ARIZ

frame structures fitted with cloth interiors. Such dwellings were highly vulnerable to fire, and many towns were, in fact, leveled by blazes. Although merchants eventually began to build their establishments of brick or stone, housing in general remained crude even in the more developed towns.

Contrary to their expectations, most miners never struck it rich. The luckiest might take out $10,000 or more in a week, and there were a few extraordinary finds, such as a single 161-pound nugget discovered in 1854. (It was valued at $30,000.) But few miners had such good fortune. Many more became ill or simply lost heart before finding any significant amounts of gold. Historians have estimated that, on average, miners earned just a few dollars a day, the amounts varying with the rise and fall of overall mine production during the decade.

The earliest mines in California were "placer" – a process in which the miner painstakingly extracted small pieces of gold from the sand and gravel in a stream. Usually this was done by swirling water and sediment in a pan, allowing whatever gold might be mixed in to sink to the bottom. Some early miners also picked gold from the cracks of boulders using nothing more than pocket knives. Faster methods of sifting gold from gravel included "rockers," "long toms," and "sluices," but, unlike panning, these methods could not be used by individuals. Rockers required two or three men; long toms, five or six; and sluices, anywhere from five to 20.

By 1851, as surface deposits began to thin out, more sophisticated methods became necessary. One of these methods involved temporarily diverting a stream and retrieving the gold from the dry bed. This could only be done in the summer, however, when the water levels were low. Another method

Above left and below: Prospectors engaged in placer mining, a process in which small pieces of gold are extracted from the sand and gravel in a stream. The advantage of this method was that it required very little capital. It was, however, time-consuming.

Above: A miner with his "rocker." This method was much faster than panning but usually required several men.

Below left: Sluices, like the one pictured here, offered another alternative to panning but required anywhere from five to 20 men.

employed in the early 1850s was hydraulic mining, in which high-powered hoses would blast away gravel from dry stream beds. The gravel was then caught in sluices where the gold could be separated out.

In addition to placer deposits, California also had quartz mines – sites where veins of gold were deeply imbedded in rock. Since deep shafts were often necessary to extract gold from these mines, it took the resources of large companies to tap into these riches. Once the ore was removed by means of picks, shovels, hand drills, and explosives, the miners would grind it into fine powder, then wash out the gold. Because of the difficulties involved, quartz mines in California produced only a small percentage of total gold mined during the 1850s.

It is estimated that, in total, California mines yielded some $600 million-worth of gold during the 1850s, but much of the action took place in the first few years of the gold rush. The peak year was 1852, when miners walked away with a total of approximately $82 million. After that the placer deposits quickly became depleted, and by 1858 most miners had either become employees of large mining companies or had departed for new territories such as Colorado and Nevada. One by one, the exuberant overnight towns they had created fell silent.

Right: A woodcut depicting early practitioners of hydraulic mining, a method in which high-powered hoses would blast gravel from dry stream beds.

Below: Mining in Jackson, California. By 1851 surface deposits had thinned out considerably, forcing miners to seek more sophisticated methods.

FAREWELL, OLD CALIFORNIA

Some restless miners had started trickling out of California in the early 1850s, but it was not until 1858 that a new gold rush commenced, this time based on reports of discoveries along the Fraser River in British Columbia. The reports were highly exaggerated, as the Sacramento *Daily Union* noted in its effort to stem the flow of men out of California: "The fortunate strikes, and large piles made, are always published, whilst not a word is said about the thousands who are unfortunate." Nonetheless, nearly 30,000 people came down with what was called "Fraser Fever" during 1858.

The rush to British Columbia soon fizzled as miners saw for themselves the sharp contrast between rumor and reality. A year later, however, two more waves of excitement swept the country, but now the rumors were more solidly grounded in fact. The new mining rushes focused on two locations: Nevada's Comstock Lode – a rich concentration of silver located about 20 miles south of present-day Reno – and newly discovered gold mines just north of Denver, Colorado.

Silver had actually been discovered on the eastern side of the Sierra Nevadas while most miners were still in California, but the discovery caused little excitement at the time. The value of gold was, after all, about 20 times that of silver, and most gold-seekers considered whatever silver they found along the way little more than a contaminating substance.

The first miners to take an interest in the silver were Allen and Hosea Grosch, Pennsylvanians who had been swept up on the original gold rush. After spending four years in California the Grosch brothers grew impatient and crossed the Sierras in search of easier pickings. In the process of looking for gold, they found the silver that earlier miners had dismissed. Times being what they were, they turned their attention to the less-precious metal and began digging for silver in earnest.

The Grosch brothers might have become rich had they lived to exploit their discovery, but in the fall of 1857 both of them fell victim to the hardships of mining life. Hosea died of blood poisoning after striking his foot with a pick; two months later Allen died of exhaustion after he was caught in a blizzard.

The following spring Henry T.P. Comstock moved into the Groschs' cabin. Although he may have learned of the silver deposits from records left in the cabin, he did not pursue them; like everyone else in the area, he was still primarily interested in gold. And in January 1859 several miners did, indeed, strike gold

Below: Miners make their way through Sonora Pass, California. By 1858 the California gold rush had long since peaked, and miners were looking elsewhere for riches.

and subsequently established the town of Gold Hill. The name was not exactly a misnomer, since the gold deposits there were substantial. But it did not reflect the nature of the truly important deposits underneath it.

In the following June two Irish miners were working about a mile outside Gold Hill when they struck silver in what would come to be known as the Ophir mine. Hearing of the new discovery, Comstock rushed to the site and informed the Irishmen that the land they were working was actually his. He was lying, but the Irishmen had no way of knowing that, and they did not strenuously dispute his assertion.

Soon other miners arrived to buy into the Ophir mine, and by August large shipments of silver ore were arriving in San Francisco. As word of the high prices paid for these shipments spread across the Mother Lode country, California miners suddenly became "stark mad for silver," as one observer put it. By the fall of 1859 the first silver-mining town had been established: Virginia City.

While Virginia City was booming, other miners were heading to the gold fields of Colorado. Miners had known there was gold in Colorado for some time, but it was only after the California diggings began drying up that large numbers of miners began heading toward the Rockies. By May of 1859 news of three discoveries near Denver had spread across the country.

Horace Greeley was among those who arrived in Colorado in time to witness the beginnings of the new gold rush. Greeley noted that Gregory's Diggings, the first significant mine in the area, had been untouched wilderness six weeks before his arrival. Now, however, the camp had 4,000 residents living in log cabins, tents, and other crude shelters. Greeley predicted the future of the Colorado mines, even in the early days of the rush. "A few," he noted, "will be amply and suddenly enriched by finding leads and selling 'claims' . . . [or] by supplying the mountains with the four apparent necessities of mining life – whisky, coffee, flour, and bacon; others by robbing the miners of their hard earnings through . . . cards, roulette and 'little joker'; but ten will come out here for gold for every one who carries back so much as he left home with, and thousands who hasten hither will lay down to their long rest beneath the shadows of the mountains."

Below: The silver-mining town of Hamilton, Nevada, in 1900.

Bottom: Grocery store in Gold Hill, Nevada.

Right: The assay office in Nevada City, California.

Previous pages: Virginia City, Nevada, the first town to emerge as a result of the silver rush.

Right: Horace Greeley, who visited Colorado during the early days of the gold rush there.

Above: Miners in a typical Colorado boom town.

Although Greeley's prediction was based on experiences miners had already had in California, the new strikes attracted former forty-niners in huge numbers. Meanwhile, easterners who had missed the California gold rush were drawn west by the new strikes. The waves of emigrants established new towns all across the Colorado gold region. Four towns grew up around Gregory's Diggings alone, and others would soon follow.

Although somewhat less significant than Nevada and Colorado, other states, including Montana, Wyoming, and Idaho, also experienced mining rushes during the 1860s. In each case, the pattern was similar to what it had been in California: towns would rapidly emerge amidst a flurry of activity, only to find that a bust almost always followed a boom.

STARK MAD FOR SILVER

Throughout 1859 a steady stream of miners poured into Nevada in hopes of finding silver, and by fall the town of Virginia City had been established. Legend has it that the town got its name when a local miner – nicknamed "Old Virginny" because of his incessant bragging about his home state – stumbled one evening while drunk, broke the bottle he was carrying, and immediately yelled out, "I baptize this spot Virginia Town." While there is no proof that this incident actually occurred, the residents of the town did, in fact, officially record the name Virginia City at just about the same time the "baptism" is supposed to have taken place – probably better corroborative evidence than exists for most Western legends.

Like many mining towns before it, Virginia City was initially a very primitive community. Miners took refuge in whatever shelter they could find or quickly build. There were a few lodges as well, but the dwellings were scarcely adequate for the fierce winter that lay ahead. By late November nearly six feet of snow had fallen on the fledgling community, and the passes through the mountains were blocked by drifts of up to 60 feet. For three months the miners weathered the storms and existed on dangerously meager supplies. But in late March the snows began to melt, supply wagons at last made it through the mountain passes, and the rush into the Comstock area began anew. The stream of miners coming into the area, wrote J. Ross Browne, a journalist on the scene, stretched "as far as the eye could see."

"In the course of a day's tramp," Browne wrote, "we passed parties of every description and colour: Irishmen, wheeling their blankets, provisions, and mining implements on wheel barrows; American, French, and German foot-passengers, leading heavily-laden horses, or carrying their packs on their shoulders; Mexicans, driving long trains of pack-mules, and swearing fearfully, as usual, to keep them in order; dapper-looking gentlemen, apparently from San Francisco, mounted on fancy horses; women, in men's clothes, mounted on mules of burros . . . [Missourians] seated on piles of furniture and goods in great lumbering wagons; whisky peddlers, with their bar fixtures and whisky on muleback, stopping now and then to quench the thirst of the toiling multitude. . . . [I]n short, every imaginable class . . . was represented in this moving pageant. It was a striking and impressive spectacle to see, in full competition with youth and strength, the most pitiable specimens of age and decay – white haired old men, gasping for breath as they dragged their palsied limbs after them in the exciting race of avarice; cripples and hunchbacks; even sick men from their beds – all stark mad for silver."

Below: Virginia City, Nevada. Legend has it that the town got its name when a local miner, nicknamed "Old Virginny" because of his constant bragging about his home state, stumbled one evening while drunk, broke the bottle he was carrying, and immediately yelled out, "I baptize this spot Virginia Town."

Overleaf: A street in Virginia City. The town eventually became so crowded as a result of the silver rush that miners were forced to spread out across Nevada.

Above: Another view of Virginia City. By the fall of 1860 more than 150 businesses, including 25 saloons, had been established in the town.

Right: A firehouse in Virginia City.

While most of these miners would end their adventure with little to show for their efforts, a few would become rich beyond their dreams. The most famous success story was that of George Hearst. He had already had some success in the California gold mines in the 1850s, but Hearst was always on the lookout for bigger opportunities. Learning of the silver strikes in 1859, he immediately set out for the Comstock region and paid $450 for a stake in the Ophir mine. Hearst eventually made millions on the investment, and thus laid the foundation on which his son, William Randolph, would build a publishing empire.

By the fall of 1860 Virginia City was home to more than 150 businesses, including 25 saloons, nine restaurants, a theater, and other establishments. The city became so crowded, in fact, that silver miners were soon spreading out across Nevada. The communities they established would eventually be numbered among the country's most interesting ghost towns.

One of the first of these towns was Austin. The first strike in the Austin area was a matter of chance. In May 1862 the keeper of a Pony Express station stumbled on a piece of quartz as he was hauling a load of wood from nearby Pony Canyon. Suspecting that the quartz contained gold, the keeper sent the rock to the Virginia City assayer. The analysis confirmed the presence of gold – and rich silver content as well.

Several days after the assayer issued his report, miners be-

gan staking claims in the area, and by July a full-fledged mining camp had been established around the Pony Express station at Jacob's Springs. Within the year the camp evolved into a town, which was named Jacobsville. This settlement flourished briefly and even temporarily became the county seat, but miners soon realized it was too far from the diggings in Pony Canyon. Another town, Clifton, was established east of the canyon, but it, too, proved to be inconvenient, and the miners finally decided to establish a community in the canyon itself. By the spring of 1863 the new town – Austin – had been chosen as the county seat, and by summer a road had been built to serve the town's 366 homes. Austin continued to grow as Virginia City became overcrowded, and by the end of 1863 its population had topped 6,000. Although no one could have foreseen it at the time – for it was mainly fortuitous – Austin was now on the brink of becoming one of the most celebrated and best-described boom towns in Western American folklore.

"Its houses are built anywhere and everywhere," wrote Samuel Bowles, a New England journalist who visited Austin in 1869. "One side of a house will be four stories, the other one or two – such is the lay of the land; not a tree, not a flower, not a blade of green grass anywhere in the town." On the other hand, according to Bowles, Austin had to its credit barbers and baths of "European standards" and a "first-class" French restaurant. Although these elegant features might seem at odds with the rough qualities of the classic boom town, Bowles felt Austin was

Left: George Hearst, father of William Randolph Hearst, was among those who struck it rich in the silver mines of Nevada in 1859.

Below: Charcoal kilns at the Modoco Mine, one of Hearst's holdings.

61

"the most representative mining town" he had seen. Such were the contradictions of many boom towns: they could indeed be at once opulent and gritty.

Another visitor to Austin in the 1860s was Mark Twain, who later wrote about the town's most famous incident in his book *Roughing It*. The incident began during town's mayoral race of 1864. The opponents, Reuel Gridley (who happened to have been Twain's childhood friend in Missouri) and Dr. H.S. Herrick, agreed that the loser of the race would carry home a 50-pound sack of flour on his shoulder.

When Gridley lost the race, he shouldered the sack of flour and proceeded to march through town, accompanied by a band and the town's entire population. After arriving home, Gridley

Pages 62-63: The town of Austin, Nevada, one of the first silver-rush communities to emerge after Virginia City.

Left: Austin, Nevada, as it appeared in 1940. By the end of 1863 the town's population was more than 6,000. The town flourished for more than a decade, despite two devastating floods.

Below: Abandoned buildings in Austin. During the 1870s the town began to suffer because of its isolation. A new rail link, completed in 1880, sparked a brief revival, but the town eventually declined as the silver mines were depleted.

Overleaf: Two views of Hamilton, Nevada.

decided to auction off the flour to benefit the United States Sanitary Commission. "The bids went higher and higher, as the sympathies of the pioneers awoke and expanded, till at last the sack was [sold] to a mill-man for $250," wrote Twain. In the spirit of the proceedings, the new owner of the flour decided to sell it again for the benefit of the same charity.

"Now the cheers went up royally," Twain wrote. The auction lasted till sundown, by which time the sack of flour had been sold to 300 different people for a grand total of $8,000. And still no one took possession of the sack.

Not to be outdone by the people of Austin, residents of Virginia City invited Gridley to move the auction to their town. The auction raised $5,000, but the citizens of Virginia City were determined to surpass the achievements of their neighbors in Austin, so the auction was resumed the next day with much fanfare. With bids coming in from other nearby mining towns, the auction eventually raised $40,000. Twain wrote that the total "would have been twice as large" had the streets been wide enough to accommodate more people.

And the story did not end there. Gridley subsequently put the same sack up for auction in Carson City and in various towns in California, and legend has it that he even eventually took it to New York. "I'm not sure of that," Twain wrote, "but I know he finally carried it to St. Louis, where . . . after selling it for a large sum . . . he had the flour baked up into small cakes and retailed

Above: Treasure City, Nevada. During the boom years of the silver rush there was a strong rivalry between Treasure City and Hamilton. By 1878, however, both towns were "insignificant and nearly depopulated," according to one journalist on the scene.

them at high prices." The grand total raised by Gridley's auctions was estimated to be $150,000.

Following the excitement of the "Sanitary Flour-Sack" affair, Austin settled back down to the "routine" bustle of a mining community. Over the next decade the town flourished in spite of two devastating floods and the town's isolation. With the nearest rail line 100 miles away, Austin's residents knew they would eventually have to establish better transportation if the town were to survive, so in 1875 Austin secured a county subsidy to build a rail connection to the Battle Mountain depot. The grant stipulated that work had to be completed within five years, but the citizens of Austin could not find a company to construct the line. Finally, with only six months to go, a company was hired, and the work was completed literally within minutes of the deadline. As hoped, the new rail connection gave Austin a reprieve, but it was only temporary. When the mines were at last depleted, nothing could prevent the town from fading away.

Another community that sprouted out of the Nevada dessert during the boom years of the 1860s was White Pine. Established by the overflow of Austin's population, White Pine "went down almost as quickly as it came up," according to Fred Hart, a newspaperman who visited it. White Pine was, in fact, an amalgam of two other communities, Hamilton and Treasure City. "At the time of my arrival," wrote Hart in 1868, "there was considerable rivalry as to which of the two camps should be the future metropolis of White Pine. The mines were marvelously rich . . . and it was evident that the district was designed to receive a large population ere long – so, of course, it must have a city." Each site had something to recommend it. Treasure City was located virtually on top of the mines, right up on the 9,000-foot mountain called Treasure Hill, while Hamilton was located near the foot of the mountain and thus had better access to a large water supply. In the end, both towns maintained equal status in the "metropolis" of White Pine.

By 1878, when Hart published his memoirs, Hamilton and Treasure City were both "insignificant and nearly depopulated camps." The few who remained, he wrote, "have clung on, hoping on, hoping ever, for a strike in the mines that shall bring a return something like the good old times of the early days." For these two towns, however, those longed-for good times would never come again.

NEW ELDORADOS

While the Nevada silver mines were booming, other prospectors were busy searching for gold in Colorado, which was then part of Kansas Territory. William Green Russell, who had come to California from Georgia in 1849, sparked the new gold rush nine years later when he discovered gold just north of Pikes Peak. Although Russell's success was modest, newspapers across the country sensationalized his strikes, and miners began pouring into the region from all over the country. The lingering effects of the financial panic of 1857 spurred the rush, and by early 1859 thousands of would-be miners headed toward the Rockies, rallying around the slogan "Pikes Peak or Bust." But, largely because of their inexperience, most of the would-be miners who came from the East had little success. The key strikes were made by a few veteran prospectors, including George A. Jackson and John H. Gregory.

Gregory uncovered almost $1,000-worth of gold in a matter of days during the spring of 1859. Shortly thereafter he sold his claim for $21,000 and disappeared from the scene. Gregory's Diggings, however, became one of the focal points of the new gold rush. By September 900 miners were taking in about $50,000 per week, and by the following summer several towns had been established in the area. The most prominent of these was called Central City, located in a gulch where the miners were concentrated. Within a few years the town had attracted several thousand people. (In this connection it is worth remembering that as late as 1870 the population of Denver itself had yet to reach 5,000.)

Although Central City attracted miners, gamblers, and prostitutes rather than the "respectable" types who lived in Denver, the town boasted a number of elegant establishments. By the early 1870s visitors could be entertained at one of several theaters and could secure a night's lodging at the Teller House, a four-story hotel named after Henry M. Teller, a lawyer and leading citizen. The hotel's 90 rooms, according to a reassuring report in the local newspaper, were "tastefully fitted with all essential conveniences. The majority are . . . without transoms, ventilation being obtained by adjustable windows. Guests may

Below: The trails leading to Pike's Peak in the 1860s.

MAP OF THE GOLD MINES AND THREE PROMINENT ROUTES LEADING THERETO.

Left, top: Miners at Gregory's Diggings during the early days of Colorado's gold rush.

Left, bottom: A view of Central City, Colorado, one of several towns that grew up around Gregory's Diggings.

Above: A street in Central City.

therefore lie down to peaceful slumbers undisturbed by apprehensions of getting their heads blown off or valuables lifted by burglars."

A year after the Teller House opened it received its most prominent guest, President Ulysses S. Grant. In honor of the president's visit the citizens of Central City paved in silver the walkway leading from the hotel to the street. (Some citizens, according to the newspaper, *The Miners' Register*, had proposed laying gold bricks instead, but it was decided that gold was far too common a substance in Central City.) The president, stated the *Register*, "was quite incredulous when told that the slabs were genuine silver."

For Central City, the visit by Grant was especially significant. Unlike many other mining towns, Central City had been strongly supportive of the Union during the war. When, in 1865, a Confederate sympathizer had expressed delight at the news of President Lincoln's assassination, a lynch mob had been formed to punish the unrepentant Rebel. In the end, cooler heads prevailed, and the accused, William Taber, was given a formal trial and a modest punishment. But the incident left no doubt about where the town's sympathies lay and helps to explain why Central City was prepared to welcome Grant so extravagantly.

Despite a devastating fire in 1874 and numerous shifts in the output of the local mines, Central City survived into the twentieth century. Gold output dropped in the mid-1860s after surface deposits became depleted, but it surged again in the 1870s with the arrival of new techniques for separating gold from rock. By the turn of the century Central City was close to being a ghost town, but it somehow struggled on until the 1930s, when its citizens launched a major restoration program. Since then, although it is still home to just a few hundred residents, hundreds of thousands of tourists have visited Central City for a taste of what Colorado's nineteenth-century boom towns were like.

Colorado was by no means the only producer of boom towns in the late nineteenth century. One memorable town to emerge during this period was located in California, not far from the Nevada border. The origins of this particular town, destined to

become one of the wildest in the West, actually date back to 1857, when a group of miners drifted east and established the settlement of Monoville. By 1859 some of the Monoville miners had grown restless and had begun looking elsewhere for gold. They found it, in a valley not far from their old diggings, just as winter was setting in. After one of the men, William S. Bodey, died in a blizzard while returning from a supply run, the others agreed that the new settlement should be named after him, although for some unknown reason the spelling was changed to "Bodie".

Bodie's mines were reasonably rich, but the community itself grew somewhat more slowly than the typical boom town. Visiting it in 1864, the journalist J. Ross Browne reported that Bodie had perhaps 20 "small frame and adobe houses" as well as one boarding house. The slow growth was due, in large part, to the fact that surface deposits were scarce. Thus it was not until 1876, with the advent of a large-scale mining operation, that real growth began. As word of the Bodie mining operation spread, miners flocked to the area to get a piece of the action, and by the spring of 1877 Bodie's population of 13,000 was served by a church, a bank, and three newspapers, as well as the usual collection of saloons, boarding houses, and stores – not to mention the inevitable, and in this case highly necessary, jail.

As the population grew, violence increased, and during just one week in 1879 six men died in gunfights. The following year the *Sacramento Bee* quoted a fictitious resident identified simply as The Bad Man from Bodie: "I'm sandstorm mixed with whirlwind . . . I was born in a powderhouse and raised in a gun factory. I'm bad from the bottom up and clean grit plumb through – I'm chief of Murdertown, and I'm dry. Whose treat is it? Don't speak all at once, or I'll turn loose and scatter death and destruction full bent for the next election." Indeed, only when the mines started to play out in the early 1880s did Bodie finally begin to quiet down.

Bodie lingered on for another 40 years or so, but by the early 1920s only a few dozen residents were left. In 1930 the town experienced a brief resurgence with the opening of several old mines, but two years later a fire swept through the community and virtually snuffed it out. Today the few remaining buildings in Bodie have been preserved as part of a state park.

Another important region for mining in the 1860s was Montana Territory, and today a number of ghost towns stand as testament to this boom. Perhaps the most famous of these is Bannack.

In the summer of 1861 veteran miner Jack White and five other prospectors ventured into the hills and valleys of what is now western Montana. (At the time it was Oregon Territory and two years later it became Idaho Territory. It would not be identified as Montana Territory until 1864.) The party had had some success that year but had temporarily abandoned their efforts when the snows came. While the various members of the party "holed up" in camps nearby, White continued exploring the region until he came upon Grasshopper Creek, a site that soon proved to be rich in gold. When the men reconvened at their old site in the spring of 1862, White told his friends of the discovery, and

Left: Tourists peer into the windows of a restored saloon in Central City.

Below: A stage coach stops outside the Grand Central Hotel in Bodie, California.

the party immediately set out for it. While they were staking their claims, White's party encountered a group of Bannack Indians, who sold the miners some venison. As a result of this encounter the men named the camp after the Indian tribe.

Soon word of the success at Bannack (also called Grasshopper Diggings) spread south to Colorado, where the placer deposits were rapidly diminishing, and by winter there were some 5,000 residents in the new town. Like other mining towns, and perhaps more than most, Bannack had its share of violence. In an attempt to minimize fights among the miners, the leaders of the town drew up the "Miners' Ten Commandments," which, among other things, limited each man to a single claim, prohibited claim jumping, and – perhaps somewhat optimistically – urged residents to honor the Sabbath.

How much effect the "Ten Commandments" may have had is debatable. "The settlement," according to one late nineteenth-century historian, "was filled with gambling houses and saloons where bad men and worse women held constant vigil, and initiated a reign of infamy which nothing but a strong hand could extirpate." The most notorious of the town's "bad men" was Henry Plummer, who at one point served as sheriff of Bannack until citizens began to notice a connection between his frequent absences and the murders and robberies that were occurring in the outlying areas. Plummer's gang soon became so brazen that even the citizens of Bannack decided they had to put a stop to it. At a secret meeting held in December 1863, they pledged to capture the outlaws, and a month later Plummer was marched to the town gallows that he himself had built.

By the end of 1864 Bannack had quieted down considerably, not only because of the elimination of Plummer and his gang but because much of its gold had been depleted. It enjoyed a brief revival in the late 1860s but nearly became a ghost-town in the 1870s. Other revivals followed in the 1890s and at the outset of World War I, but by the late 1930s it was again approaching ghost-town status. Like so many former boom towns, it survives today only as a tourist attraction.

Another once-important Montana mining camp was Virginia City (not to be confused with its namesake in Nevada). The mines that gave rise to Virginia City were discovered in 1863 by five men who had been working at Grasshopper Gulch. Impatient with their progress in Bannack, the men set out for the Yellowstone in the spring of 1863. By the end of April their journey was progressing uneventfully, but on May 1 they found themselves surrounded by a party of Crow Indians. Clearly outnumbered, the miners decided to surrender.

There have been several accounts of what happened after the miners were taken captive. According to one legend, the Indians simply let their prisoners go after one of the miners, Bill Fairweather, impressed them by seizing a snake in his bare

Pages 74-75: Abandoned buildings in Bodie. The town reached its peak in the late 1870s, when the population topped 13,000.

Pages 76-77: Another view of Bodie, which became increasingly violent with the influx of miners. Eventually it became known as one of the wildest towns in the West.

Below: Bannack, Montana, also known as Grasshopper Diggings.

NEW ELDORADOS

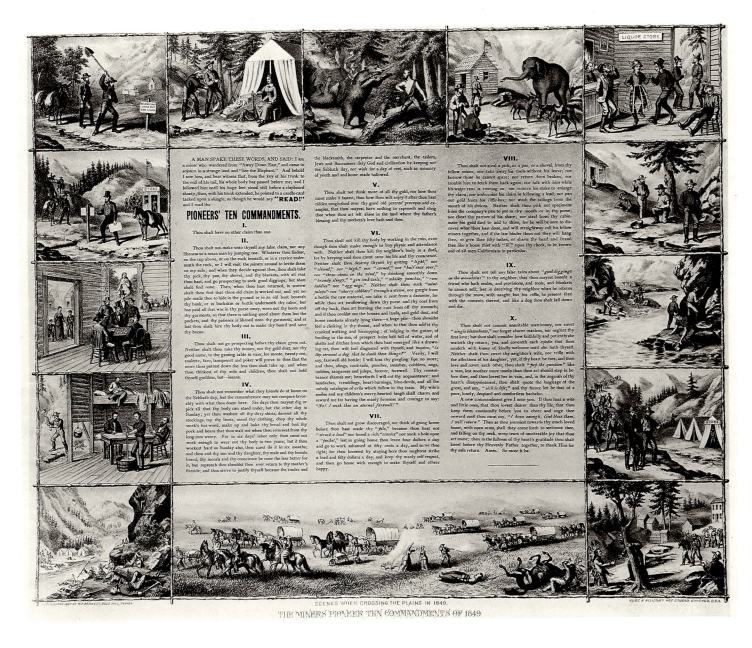

Above: The Miner's Ten Commandments. Variations on this document could be found in mining towns throughout the West during the latter half of the 19th century.

Left: An unidentified man gazes upon the grave of Henry Plummer, Bannack's most notorious outlaw.

hands. Another account involves an old squaw who befriended the miners and helped them escape. In any event, the miners were free again by May 26, according to the diary of another miner in the party, Henry Edgar, and that very same day the men struck gold.

"I had [my] pan more than half panned down and had seen some gold as I ran the sand around," Edgar wrote, "When Bill sang out, 'I have found a scad.' I returned for answer, 'If you have one I have a hundred.' He then came down to where I was with his scad. It was a nice piece of gold. Well, I panned the pan of dirt and it was a good prospect; weighed it and had two dollars and forty cents; weighed Bill's scad and it weighed the same. Four dollars and eight cents! Pretty good for tobacco money."

In the coming weeks the new diggings would yield a lot more than tobacco money. Not long after the discovery, two other miners, not of the original party, panned some $2,000 in one day, and by the end of the camp's first year the mines had yielded well over $10 million.

By January 1864 Virginia City had been incorporated and was growing rapidly, at the expense of Bannack and other nearby towns. In the following August the town acquired a newspaper, the Montana *Post*. "Though our city is but a year old," stated the paper on August 27, "fine and substantial buildings have been erected, and others are rapidly going up. One hundred buildings are being erected each week in Virginia City and environs.... Indeed, the whole [town] appears to be the work of magic – the vision of a dream."

Life in Virginia City was hardly a dream, however. Not long after Plummer's demise in Bannack, another outlaw emerged to take his place. Ironically, Jack Slade had been one of vigilantes who hunted Plummer down. Slade's own reputation for ruthlessness was established in part by Mark Twain, who wrote about the outlaw in *Roughing It*. While traveling West, according to Twain, Slade got into an argument with a wagon driver. Both men drew revolvers, but the driver was quicker. Facing a cocked gun and the choice of humiliation of death, Slade "said it was a pity to waste life on so small a matter, and proposed that the pistols be thrown on the ground and the quarrel settled in a fist fight. The unsuspecting driver agreed, and threw down his pistol – whereupon Slade laughed at his simplicity, and shot him dead!"

In the East, Slade's flagrant disregard of justice would undoubtedly have sent him to the gallows, but in the West it landed him a job as a guard with the Overland Stage Company. Judged

Top right: Main Street in Bannack, as it appeared in 1920. Today the town survives only as a tourist attraction.

Right and below: Two views of Virginia City, Montana, which was established in 1863. A year later, the town's newspaper bragged about Virginia City's "fine and substantial buildings."

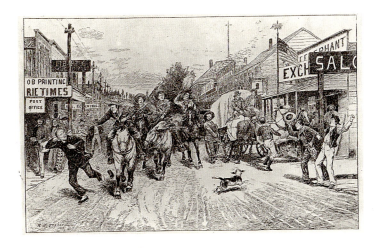

Above: Outlaws terrorize a typical Western town. In the absence of well-established law-enforcement agencies, citizens had little choice but to resort to vigilantism. The vigilantes of Montana were among the most famous in the West.

Below: A stagecoach in Ruby City.

solely in terms of pure expedience, the selection proved to be a good one: Slade quickly put an end to raids on the stage coach. But the line between law and lawlessness was blurry in the West, and Slade could be counted on only to play on whichever side suited him at the moment.

In the spring of 1863, having lost his job with the stage coach, Slade arrived in Virginia City. "He . . . might often be seen galloping through the streets, shouting, yelling, firing revolvers," wrote Thomas J. Dimsdale, then a resident of Virginia City and later the author of *The Vigilantes of Montana*. While on these sprees, he would commit considerable vandalism. "For his wanton destruction of goods and furniture, he was always ready to pay, when sober, if he had the money; but there were not a few who regarded the payments as small satisfaction for the outrage, and these men were his personal enemies."

The beginning of the end for Slade, according to Dimsdale, came one night when the outlaw and his followers got drunk and again set out to shoot up Virginia City. The sheriff of the town moved in quickly and attempted to arrest Slade but then backed off, realizing that he was hopelessly outnumbered. The

incident might have ended there, but Slade continued to press his luck. Storming into Virginia City's new courthouse, he put a gun to the judge's head and took him hostage as insurance against any further interference from the law.

When word of the incident spread, angry citizens from nearby towns marched to Virginia City to join the town's vigilance committee, and soon hundreds of vigilantes had surrounded the courthouse. Realizing he was defeated, Slade begged the vigilantes for forgiveness. But while many of the townsmen half-admired Slade, their desire for order came first. In this atmosphere of ambivalence, Slade was subsequently hanged, and "died almost instantaneously," according to Dimsdale.

By the end of the 1860s the boisterous years were over, and Virginia City's population had dropped from 10,000-plus to approximately 2,500. The town struggled on, sustained by agriculture and small-scale mining, but by the turn of the century, the population had dropped to under 400. Subsequently, however, the town restored numerous buildings, and today tourists who visit the town may see for themselves what Rank's Drug Store and Bale of Hay Saloon or the Variety Theater looked like in their prime.

The 1860s also brought mining booms to the region south of Montana, in present-day Idaho, Wyoming, and South Dakota. Catholic missionaries had known of Idaho's mining potential for almost two decades, but the Nez Perce Indians had always managed to prevent a white invasion. The turning point came in 1859, when a trader named Captain E.D. Pierce gained the Indians' trust and subsequently began prospecting along the Clearwater River. It was not long before Pierce found gold, and within months the region was teeming with miners. The Indians

Top and above: Two views of Silver City, Idaho, as it appeared in 1918. Although the town's mines yielded gold as well as silver, its fortunes began to decline in the 1870s. A brief resurgence in mining a decade later gave its remaining residents new hope, but by the early part of this century it was well on its way to becoming a ghost town.

did their best to keep the spread of white settlements in check, but their cause was hopeless. Their occasional small victories notwithstanding, they ultimately were subdued, just as so many other tribes had been in previous decades.

Two significant towns to emerge during Idaho's mining boom were Ruby City and Silver City, both located in the Owyhee

Basin, west of Boise. Established in 1863, Ruby City seemed destined for greatness. A reporter for the Boise *News* reported in 1864 that the town was alive with the sounds of "whips popping, hammers knocking . . . anvils ringing, miners singing, horses running, (with fellows on'em), and bull-drivers swearing." What was more, he added, the Pony Express had made two successful trips to the new town, bringing San Francisco newspapers that were "only seven days old." The only "seedy individuals" in Ruby City, the reporter concluded, were lawyers. In all, the town had a population of about 1,000 toward the end of 1864.

Meanwhile, Silver City had been established somewhat closer to the area's mines, and it soon became clear that the newer town would overshadow Ruby City. In large part because of its superior location, Silver City gradually lured residents away from Ruby City, and by 1866 the county seat had been transferred from the latter to the former.

Silver City's mines yielded gold as well as silver, but, as the town's name implies, silver was present in far greater quantities. One of the town's mines, for example, yielded some $7,000 in silver and about $800 in gold per ton of rock. These were promising figures, and over the next few years the mining operations in Silver City throve. By 1870, however, the production of the mines began their inevitable downturn, and before long, according to the Boise *Statesman*, miners were abandoning their pursuit of gold and silver in favor of "the more permanent pursuits of farming and stock breeding." A decade later, Silver City experienced a resurgence in mining, and some of the newer operations remained productive well into the twentieth century. But mining could not sustain the town forever, and by the early 1940s Silver City had become a ghost town.

Wyoming was another region where gold had been discovered as early as the 1840s, but there, too, the mining boom was delayed by Indian resistance. Not until 1866, when federal troops were stationed in the area, did prospectors feel safe enough to begin searching for gold, and by the summer of 1867 they had found it. Almost overnight the area's first boom town – South Pass City – became a flourishing community of several thousand residents.

Just as the Nez Perce Indians had in Idaho, the Sioux Indians in Wyoming (then part of Dakota Territory) remained a threat to individual whites, if not an obstacle to white settlement in general. Skirmishing between miners and Indians escalated steadily, and by 1869 Indian raids on freight wagons and on some of the smaller camps around Southern Pass City had become a matter of real concern.

But while most of the residents of South Pass City were preoccupied with Indian raids, one citizen had another kind of battle on her mind – the fight for women's rights. In 1869 Mrs. Esther Morris persuaded the candidates for the territorial legislature to pledge that if elected they would introduce a bill giving women the right to vote. W.H. Bright, a Republican, won the election and followed through on his pledge. The bill not only

Below: South Pass City, Wyoming. Gold had been discovered in Wyoming as early as the 1840s, but Indian resistance delayed the mining boom until 1866, when federal troops arrived.

647 South Pass, Fremont Co., Wyo.

gave women the right to vote for the first time in United States history, it allowed them to hold public office, and Mrs. Morris thus became America's first elected female justice of the peace.

By the early 1870s the placer deposits around South Pass City were getting thin. Consequently, when an expedition led by General George Custer discovered gold in the Black Hills of present-day South Dakota in 1874, Wyoming's mining activity rapidly declined. By 1875 the town of Deadwood, South Dakota had emerged, and a year later it was a roaring town of 25,000 residents, among whom was James Butler Hickok.

Wild Bill Hickok's story embodies both the romance and gritty reality of the American West in the late nineteenth century. Born in 1837 in Illinois, Hickok had gone to Kansas as a young man. After serving with distinction as an Army scout during the Civil War and for several years afterward, he made his living as a professional gambler and a U.S. marshal. By all accounts, he did indeed engage in some of the kinds of classic showdowns that are depicted in westerns. But his battles were not always noble: in 1871 he was fired from his job as marshal in Abilene, Kansas, after engaging in a gunfight more befitting a hot-tempered "shootist" than a professional lawman. In any event, by the time he arrived in Deadwood his glory days were behind him. Worn down by drinking and suffering from eye trouble, he was no longer the fierce gunfighter the public had heard so much about. Yet his reputation was still intact, and because it was, it would be his downfall.

One afternoon, a man named Jack McCall walked up behind Hickok at a poker table and without warning shot him in the head. He was seeking revenge for the death of his brother, whom Hickok had supposedly killed. McCall was later hanged, but before walking to the gallows he was reportedly asked why he had acted in such a cowardly way. The answer was simple: to challenge Hickok face to face, McCall said, would have been "suicide." Such were the dangers of having a deadly reputation in Deadwood in the 1870s.

Unlike South Pass City, which withered away after its mining boom, Deadwood survived to see calmer times. In its twentieth-century incarnation it is nothing like it was when Wild Bill Hickok passed through. But the ghosts of the old Deadwood still wander through the rooms of the many historic buildings the town has so lovingly preserved.

Previous page: South Pass City, as it appeared in 1903.

Above: Wild Bill Hickok, who was shot in the back while playing poker in a Deadwood, South Dakota, saloon. Asked later why he did not have the guts to challenge Hickok face to face, the killer said that to do so would have been "suicide."

Below: A view of Deadwood in 1888. Many of its historic buildings have been preserved.

Right: Miners working outside of Deadwood.

RUSTLERS, RASCALS, AND RAILROADERS

"The Americans have a perfect passion for railroads," wrote the French economist Michel Chevalier in the 1830s. He was not wrong, but even he might have been surprised by what was coming. By the time the California gold rush began, the nation's railroad workers had lain 9,000 miles of track. A decade later the network totalled 30,000 miles. The Civil War brought further railroad development. Though the nation added only about 5,000 miles of track during the war, railroad technology advanced enormously, and in the years following the war the industry experienced a fantastic surge in growth. It was not until the panic of 1893, by which time more than 165,000 miles of line were in operation, that construction slowed, and by then many a town had already come and gone as a direct result of the "iron horse."

But before the railroad towns – and in a sense their precursors – had been the communities that grew up along the Santa Fe and Oregon Trails. Never as elaborate as the railroad towns, these trail towns sometimes had equally colorful histories. One such was Diamond Springs, a key stop on the way to Santa Fe.

The town site first attracted white settlers after Major George Sibley came upon a large fresh-water spring there. "The spring . . . furnishes the greatest abundance of most excellent, cold water – enough to supply an army," Sibley wrote in 1839. Over the next decade Diamond Springs became increasingly popular as a rendezvous point where small groups of travelers could hook up with wagon trains. By 1849 the town had several large buildings, one of which was a hotel, and several corrals for livestock. It appeared to travelers to be a perfect haven along an otherwise dangerous trail.

In reality, the town was all too vulnerable to Indian attack. One afternoon in the fall of 1852, for example, U.S. Dragoons encamped east of the town were startled by the sight of a prairie fire that had been set by members of the Kaw tribe. "A stiff gale was blowing from the south, and when we noticed it, the fire in the tall grass was roaring furiously and the flames were leaping twenty feet high," wrote Col. Percival G. Lowe. "Every man

Railroad workers and onlookers celebrate the historic meeting of the Central Pacific and Union Pacific Railroads at Promontory, Utah, on May 10, 1869.

used a gunny sack or saddle blanket and worked with desperate energy," Lowe recalled. After about 15 minutes the fire was extinguished, but "the battle left scars on nearly all."

Such incidents were not uncommon during the 1850s, and the following decade brought more violence still. It culminated in 1863, when the area surrounding Diamond Springs was infiltrated by a gang of outlaws. On May 5 the gang raided the town itself, robbing the general store and killing its owner. The town had been failing for some time anyway, since traffic along the Santa Fe Trail had been diminishing, but this burst of wanton violence seems to have been the last straw. In the aftermath of the raid the town was abandoned, and today the site is marked only by a few ruins.

Not all the violence that plagued Kansas towns was perpetrated by Indians and outlaws. Many towns were marred by clashes between pro-slavery and anti-slavery forces in the years leading up to the Civil War. The town of Franklin was among them. Franklin was established in 1853, and when Kansas was declared a territory a year later, numerous Southerners moved there. Because of its proximity to the anti-slavery town of Lawrence, conflict in the area was inevitable. "I have my rifle, revolver, and old home-stocked pistol where I can lay my hand on them in an instant," wrote Col. A.J. Hoole, who lived just outside of Franklin. "I take this precaution to guard against the midnight attacks of the Abolitionists, who never make an attack in open daylight. . . . "

The first serious clash came in May of 1856 when pro-slavery forces vandalized Lawrence and burned a hotel there. A few weeks later, citizens of Lawrence launched a counterattack against Franklin. The battle ended with one dead and six wounded. Trouble resumed in August after D.S. Hoyt of Lawrence was murdered just outside of town. Hoyt had just come from a meeting at a pro-slavery camp where the was attempting to negotiate a truce between the two sides. When word of Hoyt's murder reached Lawrence, 75 men banded together for another attack on Franklin. After an exchange of gunfire, the anti-slavery men set fire to a building in which their enemies had taken cover. The pro-slavery forces eventually surrendered, and the citizens of Lawrence marched back to their town in triumph.

Although the battle did not immediately put an end to trouble

Above: A stone house built in Franklin, Kansas, in 1857. The house, which no longer exists, was one of the last remaining structures on the old townsite.

Below: Col. Edwin Vose Sumner arrived in Lecompton, Kansas, from his post at Fort Leavenworth, in an attempt to keep peace between pro-slavery and anti-slavery forces.

Above: Massachusetts Street in Lawrence, Kansas. Lawrence, now a bustling university town, was an anti-slavery stronghold in the mid-19th century. Its proximity to Franklin, a pro-slavery community, made conflict in the area inevitable.

Below: A mock hanging in Hunnewell, Kansas. In 1880, Hunnewell began to flourish as the terminus for the St. Louis, Kansas and Southwestern Railroad, but by 1893 its decline had begun. Today only a few buildings remain.

Below: A street in Lawrence, Kansas, in 1860.

Above: The "Grandma Bloom" house in Peterton, Kansas. Peterton flourished after coal beds were discovered there in the early 1870s, but by the turn of the century the town's best days were behind it.

in the area, it did severely undermine pro-slavery morale and Southern sympathizers eventually left Franklin altogether. By the time war came, Franklin had become an anti-slavery stronghold and a haven for runaway slaves.

After the war Franklin experienced rapid decline, and by 1867 the town was virtually dead. Today a single abandoned farmhouse is the only remaining evidence of Franklin's existence.

Another Kansas town marred by violence in general, and clashes over slavery in particular, was Black Jack. In fact, in the spring of 1856 John Brown himself had led an attack against pro-slavery forces which had been terrorizing the town. But in the end, like Franklin, Black Jack's ultimate fate would be tied to the traffic along the Santa Fe Trail. When stage and wagon traffic slowed, the town began to decline. It was finally abandoned altogether when the Santa Fe Railroad missed it by several miles, and today nothing remains of Black Jack save a park which marks the site of John Brown's attack.

As towns along the Santa Fe Trail faded into history, more and more railroad towns began to emerge. One of these was Sheridan, Kansas, which served as the Kansas Pacific Railroad's terminus between 1868 and 1870. Named after General Philip Sheridan, who had visited the townsite early in its development, the town was built on the east bank of the Smoky Hill River. "Sheridan is situated on the side of a desolate ravine," wrote W.F. Webb, a reporter for *Harper's* magazine, in 1868. "A month's hammering and the new town was built. Before one street had been surveyed, however, the engineer was called upon to locate a graveyard." A week later, Webb reported, the cemetery had three "inhabitants," all of whom had been murdered. It was an appropriate beginning for a town that was to be marked by extreme violence throughout its brief history.

To combat the outlaws who terrorized Sheridan, local businessmen formed a vigilance committee which immediately hanged three men suspected of crimes. Over the next two years 27 other men would die at the hands of these vigilantes.

As if outlaws were not enough, Indian raids posed another danger. One visitor in 1868 reported that the town was "in a state of siege," having been attacked several days prior by "a large party of savages... [who] appeared on two buttes near the town and opened fire upon the inhabitants. Everybody rushed to arms, and for the larger part of the day a spirited fusilade [sic] was kept up."

Yet some visitors professed to see some good in Sheridan. A reporter for the *Kansas Weekly Tribune* wrote in 1868 that the town was "a lively, stirring place. The customs and ways of the town are rather on the free and easy, high-pressure order and there is but little danger of the citizens dying from ennui. Whiskey, tents, gamblers, roughs, and 'soiled doves' are multiplying at an astonishing rate and all things are lively indeed."

A year later, another journalist called Sheridan "a gay village

Above: Chinese laborers travel on a section of Northern Pacific track.

Below: Residents of Peterton gather near the town's coal mine shortly after an engine explosion in 1896.

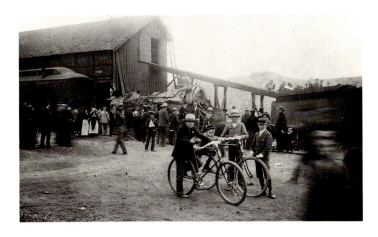

with fine wide streets" and numerous "dance halls." The town was safe, this reporter concluded, so long as one minded one's own business. "Delicate inquiries into matters which belong to your neighbor are not healthy."

The town's population, according to a third journalist, consisted mostly of "able-bodied" men, few of whom were over 30 years old. He wrote, "they have a restless, uncertain look and a quickness of movement both strange and familiar...."

In the spring of 1869 the Kansas Pacific Railroad formally announced plans to extend its line to Denver, and by late summer Kit Carson, Colorado, had become the railroad's terminus. A year later, only 80 people were left in Sheridan, and by 1875 Sheridan was a ghost town, with only the stationhouse remaining. An "air castle could not have faded out more completely than has this air town," wrote Webb that year. Today even the stationhouse has disappeared; what remains of this "lively, stirring place" is a pasture.

Another town linked to rail development in Kansas was Peterton, located about 25 miles south of Topeka. When coal beds were discovered there in the early 1870s, T.J. Peter, a manager for the Santa Fe Railroad, purchased the future townsite. By the middle of the decade several mining companies had begun operations there, and a branch line of the railroad had been constructed.

Although Peterton flourished as a result of this activity, it seems not to have been very inviting to outsiders. "The houses are not kept well painted, the fences are tumble down and everything looks unpleasant and uncomfortable," wrote a reporter for the *Topeka State Journal* in 1887. Yet the town kept on growing, reaching a peak population of about 600 in 1891. By the end of the decade, however, the boom was ending; by 1910 Peterton's post office and many of its businesses had closed; and by the time of the Great Depression, the place had become a ghost town. Only a few of its original structures remain standing today.

Above and below: Views of Abilene, Kansas, in the late 1870s, several years after its boom had ended. The town's boom began in 1867 after an enterprising Illinois native turned it into a cattle depot. It thrived for about four years until the railroad moved on. Its part in the legend of the Wild West makes it a popular tourist attraction today.

While Peterton and other Kansas towns were thriving as a result of the Santa Fe Railroad, the Northern Pacific Railroad was spurring the development of towns in Washington state. One such community was Roslyn, founded in the fall of 1886 after word got out that coal had been discovered in the region. Within a matter of months the town had several hundred residents from as far away as Europe. Two years after it was established, Roslyn was nearly wiped out by a fire, but the railroad valued the site enough to rebuild the town. But then the community fell victim to a bitter labor conflict from which it never fully recovered. The town survives to this day, but as a shadow – or perhaps ghost – of its former self.

Railroads would have played a key role in the opening of the West if they had never transported anything more than people and precious metals. But of course they carried many other kinds of goods and commodities as well, and of these, none was more important to the West than cattle. The Western plains had, for many decades, appeared to be a desolate landscape where nothing of great agricultural value could survive. Only gradually did Americans come to realize that these vast stretches of land were perfectly suited to cattle ranching. No one knows exactly what sparked this realization. Legend has it that shortly after the Civil War a government wagon train was abandoned after being caught in a blizzard in Wyoming. The following spring the driver returned to look for his cargo. He assumed his oxen would be dead, but to his surprise he found them alive and well: the inescapable conclusion was that their survival was due to the fact that they had been living off the wild grasses that had previously been ignored by westward travelers.

Whatever the validity of the story, there is no doubt that soon after the Civil War more and more enterprising men – men who might otherwise have gone in search of gold – went into ranching. And one by-product of this new development was the sudden emergence of the classic Western cattle town.

The first important cow-town was Abilene, Kansas, and the force behind the town was Joseph G. McCoy, an Illinois native

who had gone to Texas after the Civil War. Struck by the huge number of cattle there, McCoy recognized the need for a depot where Southwestern cattlemen could sell their herds to Northern buyers. The need for such a town was great, since thieves often harassed Texas cattlemen along the trails. But cattle driving was hard enough, even without outside interference. "There are few occupations in life," wrote McCoy, "wherein a man will hold by so brittle a thread a large fortune as by droving. In fact, the drover is nearly as helpless as a child, for but a single misstep or wrong move and he may lose his entire herd...."

McCoy tried for some time to interest various towns along the Santa Fe Railroad in becoming cattle depots, but he found no takers. Usually the town leaders regarded him "as a monster threatening calamity and pestilence," he recalled. Then he set his sights on Abilene.

"Abilene in 1867 was a very small, dead place, consisting of about one dozen log huts, low, small rude affairs, four-fifths of which were covered with dirt for roofing; indeed, but one shingle roof could be seen in the whole city. The business of the burg was conducted in two small rooms, mere log huts, and of course the inevitable saloon, also a log hut, could be found." McCoy realized, however, that this modest settlement had a lot to offer. The country, he wrote, "was entirely unsettled, well watered, [with] excellent grass...." Within two months after his arrival McCoy had organized the construction of a shipping yard, a barn, an office, and "a good three-story hotel." McCoy then sent out a publicity agent to spread news of the town's transformation. Before long herds were heading toward Abilene, and by the end of 1867 some 35,000 head of cattle had been shipped through the town.

Abilene's boom lasted about four years, but when the railroad moved farther West other cow-towns overshadowed it. In 1871 McCoy himself moved on to Newton, about 25 miles due north of Wichita, just as the Atchison, Topeka, and Santa Fe Railroad was reaching it. McCoy once again orchestrated the construction of stockyards, though this time he built them a mile-and-a-half outside of town to make life more pleasant for Newton's residents. In the course of a month Newton was transformed from a settlement of about a dozen dwellings into "quite a large town," according to one cowboy on the scene. It looked as though McCoy was about to become the new Abilene.

Saloons accounted for much of the town's size. In all, there were more than two dozen, and life, as a result, was rarely peaceful. "The firing of guns in and around town was so continuous that it reminded me of a Fourth of July celebration" recalled one resident. "There was shooting when I got up and when I went to bed."

When the cowboys weren't raising hell, they were likely to be visiting prostitutes. "You may see young girls not over 16 drinking whisky, smoking cigars, cursing and swearing until one almost loses the respect they should have for the weaker sex," wrote a reporter for *The Wichita Tribune*. "I heard one of the townsmen say that he didn't believe there were a dozen virtuous women in town."

In spite of all its excitement, Newton's boom lasted only one year. Afterward, the town settled into quiet respectability, just as Abilene had.

The most famous cow-town of them all was of course Dodge City. Prior to 1876, when the first shipment of cattle left Dodge, this legendary town had been a shipping center for buffalo

Below: Dodge City, Kansas. Initially the town served as a shipping center for buffalo hides, but by the late 1870s it was being promoted as "the cowboy capital of the world."

hides. But when cattle business picked up, Dodge began promoting itself as "the cowboy capital of the world," where one could find "remarkably fine" grass, plenty of water, and two drinks for a quarter. Before long Dodge had been transformed into the very symbol of the Wild West, a place where lawlessness ruled, despite the presence of such legendary lawmen as Bat Masterson and Wyatt Earp.

The gaudy legends associated with Dodge City guaranteed that the town would live on as a tourist attraction long after the heyday of the cowboy was over, but many another cow-town faded into obscurity or pure ghostliness. Hunnewell, Kansas, for example, emerged just a few years after Dodge City and throve as the terminus of the St. Louis, Kansas & Southwestern Railroad. (The town was named after the railroad's president.) By the summer of 1880, when the railroad arrived, Hunnewell was flourishing, and by August the town's crown jewel, a 33-room hotel, had been constructed at a cost of $5,000. The town's greatest days, however, did not come until the early 1890s, when the government ordered all cattle removed from the nearby Cherokee Strip, which marked the boundary between Kansas and Indian Territory. As a result of the order, thousands of head of cattle were shipped through Hunnewell.

Even at its peak, Hunnewell had only 250 permanent residents – a tiny population compared to that of the mining in the far west – but like other cow-towns, Hunnewell had a relatively enormous transient population. Nevertheless, residents, both "permanent" and temporary, began to leave Hunnewell after the Cherokee Strip was opened to white settlers in 1893. The town straggled into the twentieth century but steadily faded, and in 1939 even the once-cherished hotel was torn down. Today only a few buildings remain.

Previous pages: A view of Front Street in Dodge City in 1878. Despite the sign warning visitors not to carry guns, Dodge had five killings that year.

Below: Dodge City in 1877. The wagonload of buffalo hides at right indicates that the business on which the town was founded did not cease after the cowboys took over.

Above: Wyatt Earp, who served as assistant U.S. marshal in Dodge City while also moonlighting as a monte dealer in the town's largest saloon, The Long Branch.

RUSTLERS, RASCALS, AND RAILROADERS

By the mid-1880s the age of the cowboy had all but ended. America's original cattle industry had been dependent on the open range, but as ever more people flocked to the West to pursue farming and other less land-consuming activities, federal laws were more strictly enforced, and large areas of public domain disappeared. The dry summer of 1886 and the harsh winter that followed it dealt further blows to the cattlemen, and though cattle ranching remained an important industry, it would never be the same as it had been in those two lively decades after the Civil War.

Left: Bat Masterson, sheriff of Ford County, Kansas, which included Dodge City. "Bat is well known as a young man of nerve and coolness in cases of danger," asserted *The Dodge City Times* when Masterson was running for sheriff. This proved to be an understatement, as Masterson went on to become a national celebrity and folk hero.

Below: Cowboys drive cattle through the heart of Dodge City. The town quieted down considerably after the golden age of the cowboy ended in the mid 1880s.

KANSAS.— RAISING SUPPLIES OF MEAT FOR FOREIGN MARKETS — A HERD OF TEXAS "LONG-HORNS" BEING DRIVEN TO THE CATTLE RENDEZVOUS, DODGE CITY.— SKETCHED BY EDWARD RAPIER.

Tonopah, Nevada, which emerged in 1900 after a man named Jim Butler discovered an outcropping of silver ore nearby.

TURN-OF-THE-CENTURY BOOM TOWNS

GHOST TOWNS

Above: Tonopah, looking south, in 1901.

Below: Goldfield, Nevada, once promoted as "the greatest gold camp ever known."

TURN-OF-THE-CENTURY BOOM TOWNS

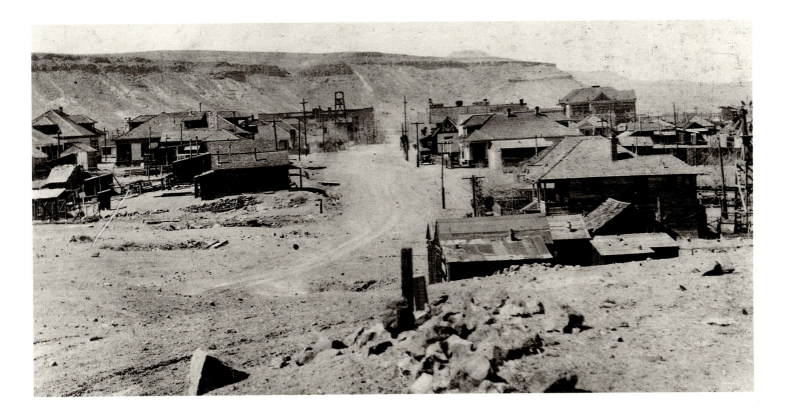

Like ranching, mining underwent a profound transformation in the 1880s. No longer was it dominated by individual prospectors. Huge companies, based in large cities on both coasts, had bought up most of the mines and had turned mining from an adventurous pursuit of riches into routine wage labor. Yet there remained some exceptions. A reappearance of the old-fashioned gold rush occurred in Nevada in the spring of 1900.

The new Nevada boom began when a man named Jim Butler discovered an outcropping of silver ore midway between Las Vegas and Reno. By fall news of Butler's discovery had spread across Nevada, then across the country, and the town of Tonopah quickly emerged. Within two years its population had hit 20,000. Meanwhile, prospectors were scouring the surrounding area for new mines. One area of particular interest was Columbia Mountain, about 25 miles south of Tonopah. In 1902 two prospectors, Harry Stimler and Billy Marsh, had gone to the mountainside after learning that a Shoshone Indian had discovered a small amount of gold ore there. Within a matter of days they had discovered enough ore to convince them that they were working "the granddaddy of all gold mines." As a result, they named their camp "Grandpa."

During its first year Grandpa appeared to be nothing more than a flash in the pan. In the spring of 1903, however, several miners hit pay dirt. One of them, Charley Taylor, struck gold in a mine Marsh and Stimler had given him after failing to find gold there themselves. During the next six years Taylor reaped more than $1.2 million from the mine. Two other miners, meanwhile, had also hit pay dirt in the area. They named their strike Combination Mine.

On the strength of these discoveries, the residents of Tonopah began to abandon the three-year-old town in favor of the area around Grandpa. Before long a new town by the name of Goldfield had been formed. By the beginning of 1904 Goldfield had a population of 1,000, and by spring it had its own newspaper – an unabashed promoter of "the greatest gold camp ever known."

For some unscrupulous individuals, Goldfield did indeed prove to be the greatest gold camp they had known. Taking

Above: Another view of Goldfield, Nevada.

Overleaf: Tonopah, as it appeared in 1903.

lowly mining jobs for wages of just a few dollars a day so they could gain access to large established mines, these men would pocket nuggets of high-grade gold as they went about their work. Some even fashioned special shirts or jackets which allowed them to carry out as much as $2,000-worth of gold each day. Within a few years the practice had become so widespread that these "high-graders" were costing the Goldfield Consolidated Mines Company upwards of $1 million annually. Even so, the mining companies and the town of Goldfield continued to thrive, for there seemed to be virtually no end to the precious ore in the area.

The wealth flowing through town sustained several elaborate drinking and gambling establishments, some of which operated around the clock. At times, recalled one miner, "you couldn't hardly notice the difference between three o'clock in the afternoon and three o'clock in the morning." Goldfield also boasted several more civilized institutions, including a public school and a court of law. To be sure, the presiding judge, E.R. Collins, was also the proprietor of a large saloon, but this fact apparently did not compromise the court's integrity.

Entertainment in Goldfield tended to go somewhat beyond the normal hellraising. Thus in 1906 the town staged a prizefight billed as "The Battle of the Century." The night before the fight, according to one local newspaper, "the streets of Goldfield were literally jammed... with a holiday crowd of persons from all parts of the country and all walks of life." Pre-fight entertainment included drilling contests and burro races. The fight itself went 42 rounds and was widely felt to have justified all its promoters' grandiose claims.

If such extravaganzas were made possible by Goldfield's enormous wealth, that same wealth would also eventually lead to the transformation of Goldfield into a truly modern mining town – one not only with telephone lines and railroad connections but organized-labor troubles as well.

The troubles began in 1907 after the Goldfield Consolidated

105

Mines Company established monopoly control over the area. Reacting to tough new regulations imposed by the company, the miners formed a union and in November went out on strike. In response, President Theodore Roosevelt sent in federal troops to restore order. At the same time, he agreed to set up a government commission to hear the miners' complaints. In the end, however, the commission turned a deaf ear to the miners, and the company merely solidified its position.

Goldfield continued to thrive for the next two decades, but by World War I it was becoming apparent that the area's mines were not, in fact, inexhaustible. The real turning point came in 1919, when the Goldfield Consolidated Mines Company abandoned the area. Fire and floods during the 1920s further devastated the town, and yet it still would not die. Today Goldfield – and Tonopah – lived on, typical small Western towns but mere shadows of the things they were.

The same cannot be said of Rhyolite, another Nevada boom town that sprang up about 70 miles south of Goldfield. Following the discovery of gold in the region in 1904, an ephemeral settlement called Bullfrog appeared; but Bullfrog soon faded away after a bigger discovery was made a few miles distant. As miners flocked to the new site, a new town was born, and the founders named it after a kind of volcanic rock that was common to the area. In addition to its rich supply of gold ore, Rhyolite had the important advantage of being located near an ample supply of fresh water, and as a result, its fortunes soared. Before long the town had a railroad station, a large hotel, three newspapers, two churches, a public school, and 45 saloons, serving more than 16,000 residents. But the boom was short-lived, by 1910 the mines were nearly depleted, and by the beginning of World War I, Rhyolite had been abandoned. Today the town exists solely in the form of a few ruins.

While Goldfield Consolidated and other large companies were tightening their grip on gold-mining operations, coal companies were establishing company towns that were even more rigid. Perhaps the most famous of these towns was Ludlow, site of one of the bloodiest labor clashes in American history.

Established by the Colorado Fuel and Iron Company, Ludlow was a typical coal-company town. Housing consisted of pitiful shanties, and an ever-present cloud of black smog blocked out the sun. Miners breathed coal dust not only during their 10-hour shifts but around the clock. Their average lifespan was 45 years.

Ludlow did sustain some businesses. By 1913 the town had two grocery stores, five saloons, a blacksmith, a general store, a bakery, a bookstore, a boardinghouse, a livery and feed store, and a doctor, not to mention a brick railroad station. This list of civic assets is somewhat misleading, however, since all were owned by the company. The company paid its workers in scrip instead of cash, thus compelling them to shop at company stores. The stores, in turn, charged exorbitant prices.

Left, top: The Mohawk Gold Mine in Goldfield.

Left, bottom: Rhyolite, Nevada, in 1908. The town was named after a kind of volcanic rock common to the region.

Below: Rhyolite's abandoned railroad station. Gold was discovered nearby in 1904, and before long a town of 16,000 had emerged. The boom was short-lived, however; by 1910, the mines were nearly depleted.

Left: Rhyolite as its appears today.

Above: Workers at the Tiera Coal Mine in California around 1905. The average lifespan of coal miners at the turn of the century was 45 years.

The first strike in response to these grim conditions had occurred in 1903, but the company had quickly put an end to the protest by bringing in strikebreakers under the protection of armed guards. Another decade would pass before the strikebreakers themselves would be driven to strike. The strike of 1913-14 involved thousands of miners from Ludlow, Segundo, and other company towns in the region. In retaliation, the Colorado Fuel and Iron Company evicted the strikers, but the mineworkers still stuck together, setting up several tent colonies, the largest of which was outside of Ludlow.

This was in September 1913. By the third week in October two people had been killed in clashes between the strikers and company guards. State militia and National Guardsmen were brought in to prevent further trouble, and the strike remained relatively quiet over the next few months. Then, one morning in

the following April, for reasons that are not entirely clear, militiamen occupied a hill overlooking the miners' camp and set off two bombs. Believing they were under attack, the miners grabbed their rifles and returned fire. The gun battle that followed lasted for the next twelve hours. One boy and three men were killed, and worse was yet to come.

Under orders from their officers, the militiamen proceeded to pour coal oil on the miners' tents and set them afire. "During the firing of the tents, the militiamen became an uncontrolled mob and looted the tents of everything that appealed to their fancy or cupidity," a government investigator wrote later. Meanwhile, women and children who had taken cover in pits underneath the tents scrambled to escape the flames. Not all of them did: in one pit, 11 children and two women suffocated or were burned to death. Several unarmed strikers who had been taken prisoner were also murdered.

As word of the massacre spread, miners from the surrounding area desended on Ludlow to battle the mining company. It was not until the end of April, when President Woodrow Wilson sent in federal troops, that the fighting ended. By then, more than 50 people had died.

Although the government investigated the massacre, coal-mining conditions improved only marginally, if at all. Ludlow survived for many years thereafter but eventually faded away as the mining operation ceased to become profitable. Today only a few buildings remain alongside a monument to victims of the Ludlow Massacre.

Because of its lack of water and its remoteness from railroad lines, Arizona had at first lagged behind most of the West in its development. The turning point came with the construction of

Above: A member of the Colorado militia mans a machine gun during the miner's strike at Ludlow in 1914. In the fall of 1913 thousands of miners began a protest of the brutal conditions imposed upon them by the Colorado Fuel and Iron Company. The strike culminated in a massacre, in which some 50 men, women, and children were shot or burned to death.

Right: Miners survey the remains of a tent colony destroyed by militiamen during the Ludlow strike.

the Southern Pacific Railroad across southern Arizona between 1878 and 1881 and then with the construction of another line to the north in 1883. (The latter eventually became part of the Santa Fe Railroad.)

As the railroads were completed in Arizona, a number of towns began to emerge. Among them was Tombstone – a silver-mining town that, along with Dodge City, has symbolized the Wild West for many generations of armchair cowboys. But symbolic or not, Tombstone was an atypical Arizona town in one respect: whereas its citizens had initially been excited by the prospect of finding silver, another metal would produce most of Arizona's mining boom towns – copper.

Copper mining itself was a late-blooming industry. It began in earnest about 1880 after Phelps Dodge, a New York import-export firm, sent Dr. James Douglas, an early expert on copper refining, to explore mining opportunities in the Southwest. Dodge had already learned of a promising copper mine at Morenci, Arizona, and Douglas soon informed them of another potentially valuable property at Bisbee, just north of the Mexican border. Acting on Douglas's advice, Dodge invested in claims at both locations. The Bisbee mine, known as the

TURN-OF-THE-CENTURY BOOM TOWNS

113

Copper Queen, turned out to be enormously profitable well into the 1900s, as well as becoming a major testing ground for improvements in the copper-mining process.

Another important mine was located in the town of Jerome, located midway between Phoenix and Flagstaff. Locals had been aware of copper deposits in the Jerome area for years, but in the absence of a railroad line, no one had been able to take advantage of the potential opportunity. When the railroad finally was completed, Territorial Governor Frederick A. Tritle proposed a large-scale operation at a site called Mingus Mountain. To help finance the venture, Tritle brought in a New York lawyer named Eugene Jerome.

By 1883 the town named after Jerome had a population of about 400, but that seemed to be about the extent of its potential. Indeed, the mine closed altogether in 1885 after copper prices fell, and Jerome might well have become a ghost town then had not William Andrews Clark, a senator from Montana, purchased the site. With unwavering faith, Clark expanded the mine, built additional housing for miners, and constructed a large hotel. And the investment paid off. By the mid-1890s Jerome's mines were again so profitable that the town's population had topped 10,000. This dramatic growth was briefly interrupted by several fires late in the decade, but after each blaze the town was rebuilt, and by the turn of the century the area's population was growing faster than ever.

It was not, however, a very attractive growth. In the valley below the town lay a huge smelter whose fumes polluted the air and killed most of the surrounding vegetation, and battered and scarred Mingus Mountain had some 85 tunnels running through it. Few people complained about these blights on the landscape as long as the mines remained profitable, which they did, well into the 1920s. But in 1925 the mining operation literally began to backfire on the town. Dynamite used to expose new deposits began causing landslides on Mingus Mountain, and many buildings started to inch their way down the mountainside, a few actually collapsing. Disaster was averted only because the townspeople reinforced their homes and businesses with cable and timber.

But before long, the town's economic fortunes would begin to slide as well. Like countless businesses across the country,

Above left and right, and below: Jerome, Arizona. Jerome emerged during Arizona's copper-mining boom of the early 1880s but did not see its true heyday until the mid-1890s, when William Andrews Clark, a senator from Montana, bought the mine and upgraded it. The mines remained profitable for several decades, but eventually closed. In spite of what the sign says, the town lingers on today, largely because of tourists who are interested in its history.

Right: A cockfight in Tombstone around 1885. Unlike many Arizona towns in the 1880s, which flourished as copper-mining centers, Tombstone grew on the strength of its silver-mining operations.

Right, below: The OK Corral in Tombstone, Arizona, site of the legendary gunfight between the Earps and the Clantons.

the mines of Jerome died during the Great Depression. The biggest reopened during World War II but closed again – probably for good – in the early 1950s. That the town still survives is in part due to tourism: as do so many other Western towns, Jerome now owes a fair portion of its livelihood to its ghosts.

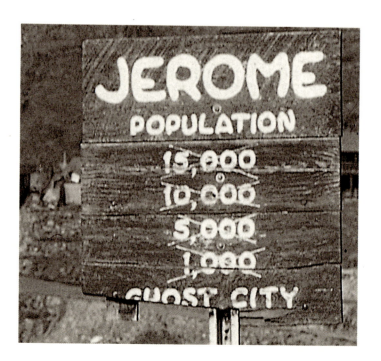

Below: The town of Seward, Alaska, in the early days of the Klondike Gold Rush.

EPILOGUE: AN ENDURING LEGACY

WANTED!
Quartz Placer Claims

A.J.BANNERMAN & CO.
MINE BROKERS
GENERAL AGENTS

POST OFFICE

The early camps of the California gold rush, Van Wyck Brooks once wrote, "were scarcely more than disorganized raids on nature that left behind battlefields strewn with waste and decay...." The same might be said of many later boom towns throughout the West. So intoxicated were nineteenth-century Americans by the natural riches of this continent that they failed to recognize its limitations. Thus they moved into territory after territory tearing up the land with mining machinery, railroad tracks, and cattle hooves, rarely considering the long-term impact of their pursuits.

The recklessness of the nineteenth century now seems to us in many ways childish: the people who built and abandoned classic boom towns did so with all the careless energy and impatience of a toddler shifting from one toy to another. But by the same token, as we tour the West today in the comfort of our air-conditioned automobiles, we find it almost impossible to imagine ourselves facing the hardships so routinely accepted by the early settlers. That they were willing and able to endure such adversity is a testament both to their entrepreneurial spirit and to the magnetic power of the landscape. The fact that there was *so much* land available made it all the more difficult to resist moving about.

Our twentieth-century world is very different from that of our forbears. The frontier closed a century ago. We live not in an agricultural or pioneering society but in an industrial – perhaps even post-industrial – society. We are vastly more aware both of threats to the environment and of the finite nature of our resources. Yet, deep down, have we changed quite as much as we should like to believe?

Certainly American towns will never again grow and die at the rate they did in the nineteenth century. But transience is still very much a part of our nature, and we still tend to favor "progress" over renewal. The Alaskan pipeline project of the 1970s is one indication that some old American attitudes may be still very much alive.

The project, initiated in 1970, was designed to channel oil from Prudhoe Bay south to Valdez. Environmentalists, fearing the pipeline would disrupt the ecological balance of the surrounding area, filed suit to stop the project. Three years later, after a compromise was struck, construction of the pipeline was finally resumed.

To accommodate the massive influx of workers needed for the pipeline, 29 camps were built along the route. One, the Isabel Pipeline Camp, built at the foot of Gulkana Glacier in the Alaska Range, housed 1,200 workers during its peak years. Then, in 1976, as the pipeline neared completion, the Isabel and other camps were abandoned.

Of course these camps were never intended to be permanent communities; workers moved there with a specific time-frame in mind. But the quick-profit money-making spirit reflected in the camps links them in some essential ways to the boom towns of the past. And they *were* raids on nature – only this time organized raids.

Not all the communities involved in the pipeline were new.

Previous pages: Residents of Dawson, Alaska await delivery of the mail. The photograph was taken around 1900.

Below: The Klondike Gold Rush differed from earlier gold rushes in several important ways, not the least of which was the strong presence of women.

EPILOGUE: AN ENDURING LEGACY

Above: Actresses bound for the Klondike around 1897.

Valdez had existed as a small town before the pipeline project and has survived the pipeline's completion. During construction, however, the town's population more than tripled with the influx of laborers, engineers, and other project workers, and inevitably this changed the town's character. Valdez, in fact, began to assume many of the aspects of an old-fashioned boom town. Saloons became a popular diversion, gamblers and prostitutes moved in to get a share of the easy money, and the incidence of crime and violence rose. No doubt some Valdez residents were willing to tolerate the disruptions in order to reap the financial benefits, but it is not hard to imagine that many were thankful when construction was completed and the population of Valdez dropped to its old level of about 3,000.

America has not seen many boom towns in recent years, but old towns do continue to die off. A town in the Midwest, for instance, was recently reported to have a population of one – all the other residents had moved to a large town nearby in search of better opportunities. And almost all of us are familiar with at least some of those little towns whose once-bustling main streets have become increasingly ghostly as a result of competition from large chain stores and shopping malls located miles away. Sooner or later there must come a time when land will become too valuable simply to abandon. But until then Americans will probably continue, as they always have, to leave places behind so that, as de Toqueville noted, they may carry their changeable longings elsewhere.

Below: Shops in Deering, Alaska, 1903.

These pages: Tugboats pull a floating dock weighing 6.5 million pounds toward the marine tanker terminal of the Alaska pipeline in Valdez. The massive influx of workers needed for the pipeline was in some ways reminiscent of the mining rushes that occurred a century earlier.

Overleaf: The ghost town of Eureka, Colorado.

Page 126: Ruins in the town of Rhyolite. While America has seen few boom towns in recent years, once-thriving communities all across the country continue to die off as their residents move on in search of better opportunities.

INDEX

Abilene, KS 86, *96*, 96, 97
Abolitionists 90, 94
Adams Express bank 25
Alaskan Pipeline 120-21, *122*
Amador County, CA 21
American River 13, 14, 17
Angel, George 29
Angels Camp 29, *29, 30, 31*
Appalachian Mountains 9
Atchison, Topeka, & Santa Fe Railroad 97
Auraria 9
Aurora, NV *6*
Austin, NV 60, 61, *62-63, 64*, 65, 65, 68

bandits 25
Bannack, MT 73, *78*, 78, *79, 80*, 80. *See also* Grasshopper Diggings.
Bannack Indians 78
Bennett, Charles 16
Bisbee, AZ 112
Black Hills (SD) 86
Black Jack, KS 94
Bodey, William S. 73
Bodie, CA 73, *73, 74-5, 76-7*
Boise *News* 83
Boise *Statesman* 83
Borthwick, J. D. 21
Bowles, Samuel 61
Brannan, Sam 17
Bright, W. H. 83
British Columbia 51
Brooks, Van Wyck 120
Brown, John 94
Browne, J. Ross 57, 73
Brundage, E. F. 34
Buffum, E. Gould 42
Bullfrog, NV 109
Butler, Jim 105

Calaveras County, CA 21, 29, *29*, 42
California 8, 10, 13, 17, 51, 52, 56, 65, 71, 73. *See also* gold rush.
Cannon, Jack 42
Carson City, NV 65
Cataldo, ID *46*
cattle 96, 97, 100, *101*, 101
"Celebrated Jumping Frog of Calaveras County" 29
Central City, CO 69, *70, 71*, 71, *72*
Central Pacific Railroad *88-9*
Cherokee Indians 9
Cherokee Strip 100
Chevalier, Michel 89
Chinese Camp, CA 30
Civil War, 86, 89, 90, 96, 97, 101
Clappe, Louise 21
Clark, William Andrews 114
Clearwater River 82
Clifton, NV 61
coal mining 94, *95*, 109, 110, 111, 112. *See also* Ludlow Massacre.

Collins, E. R. 107
Coloma, CA 21, 23, *24*, 28
Colorado 50, 51, 52, 56, 69, *69*, 71, 71, *72*, 78
Colorado Fuel and Iron Company 109, 111, 112
Colorado militia in Ludlow Massacre, 111-12, *112*
Columbia, CA 29, 30, 31. *See also* Hildreth's Diggings.
Columbia Mountain (NV) 105
Combination Mine 105
Comstock Lode 51, 57
Comstock, Henry T. P. 51
copper mining *1*, 112, 114, *114, 115*
Copper Queen mine 113-14
Coulterville, CA *40*
cowboys 97, 100, *100, 101*, 101
Crow Indians 78
Custer, George 86

Dawson, AK *120*
Deadwood, SD *86*, 86, *87*
Deering, AK *121*
Denver, CO 51, 52, 69, 95
Diamond Springs, KS 89, 90
Dimsdale, Thomas J. 81, 82
Dodge City, KS *97*, 97, *98-99*, 100, *100, 101*, 112
Dodge City Times 101
Dodge, Phelps 113
Douglas, James 113
Downie, William 33
Downieville, CA 33, *35*, 42
Dry Diggings, CA 21, *25*. *See also* Placerville.

Earp, Wyatt 100, *100*
Edgar, Henry *79*
El Dorado County, CA 21
Eureka, CO *124-25*

Fairweather, Bill 78
Fitzgerald, Dan 8
Flagstaff, AZ 114
Foreign Miners' Tax Law 44
Forty-Niners *19, 23, 36*
Franklin, KS 90, *90*, 94
"Fraser Fever" 51
Fraser River (BC) 51
Frémont, John C. *32*, 32, 33

gambling, 44, *44*
Georgetown, CA *8*
Georgia 9
Ghost Towns of Kansas 8
Gillespie, Charles B. 21
Gold Canyon, NV *10*
Gold Hill 52, *52*
Goldfield Consolidated Mines Company 105, 109
Goldfield, NV *104, 105*, 105, 109, *109*

gold rush: British Columbia 51; California 9, 13-17, *14, 17, 18-20*, 21-52, 89; Colorado 51, 52, 56, *56*, 69, *69, 70, 71, 72;* Idaho *81*, 82, *82*; Klondike *116, 120, 121;* Montana 73, 78-82, *78-81;* Nevada *104*, 105, *105*, 106-07, *108*, 109, *109*, 110; Wyoming 83, *83, 84-85*, 86
"Grandma Bloom" house *94*
Grandpa, NV 105
Grant, Ulysses S. 71
Grasshopper Creek, MT 73
Grasshopper Diggings, MT 78, *78*. *See also* Bannack.
Grasshopper Gulch, MT 78
Greeley, Horace 52, 56, *56*
Gregory, John H. 69
Gregory's Diggings, CO 52, 56, 69, *70*
Gridley, Reuel 65, 68
Grosch, Allen, 51
Grosch, Hosea 51
Gulkana Glacier, AK 120

Hamilton, NV *52, 66-67*, 68
Hangtown 21, *25*, 42. *See also* Placerville.
Harper's magazine 94
Hart, Fred 68
Harte, Bret 29, *30*
Hearst, George 60, *61*
Hearst, William Randolph 60
Herrick, H. S. 65
Hickok, James Butler "Wild Bill" *86*, 86
Hildreth, Thaddeus 29
Hildreth's Diggings 29
Hoole, A. J. 90
Hornitos, CA *41*, 42
housing 46, *47*, 48, 61
Hoyt, D. S. 90
Hunnewell, KS *91*, 100
hydraulic mining 50, *50*

Idaho 56, *81*, 82, *82*
Idaho Territory 73
Independence, MO 9
Isabel Pipeline Camp, AK 120

Jackson, CA *50*
Jackson, George A. 69
Jacobsville, NV 61
Jacob's Springs, NV 61
Jefferson, Thomas 9
Jerome, AZ 114, *114, 115*

Kansas Pacific Railroad 94, 95
Kansas 89-101
Kansas Territory 69
Kansas Weekly Tribune 94
Kaw Indians 89

Kit Carson, CO 95
Klondike gold rush *116, 120, 121*

Lake Tahoe 25
Las Vegas, NV 105
Lawrence, KS 90, *91, 92-93*
Lecompton, KS *90*
Louisiana Purchase 9
Lowe, Percival G. 89
"Luck of Roaring Camp" 29, 30
Ludlow, CO 109, 111, *112*, 112
Ludlow Massacre 111-12, *112, 113*
lynching *40*, 40, 42, 43, 44, 71

McCall, Jack 86
McCoy, Joseph G. 96-7
Madera County, CA 21
Madison, James 9
Manifest Destiny 10
Mariposa County, CA 21
Mariposa, CA 32, *32*, 33, *33, 34*
Mariposa County Museum and History Center 33
Mariposa Gazette office *32*
Marsh, Billy 105
Marshall, James W. *13*, 13, 14, 16, *17*, 25
Masterson, Bat 100, *101*
Merced Mining Company 32
Mexican War 10, 17
Mexicans 13, 40, 41, 42, *43*, 43, 44, 57
"Miners' Ten Commandments" 78, *79*
Mingus Mountain, AZ 114
Missouri River 10
Modoco Mine 61
Mohawk Gold Mine *108*
Mokelumne, CA 28, 46
Mokelumne River *28*
Monoville, CA 73
Montana *Post* 80
Montana 56, 73, 78-82, *78-81*
Montana Territory 73
Morenci, AZ 112
Morris, Esther 83, 86
Mother Lode region 21, *23*, 29, 32, *32*, 42, 52
Murieta, Joaquin 42, 43, *43*, 44

Nevada City, CA *53*
Nevada County, CA 21, *38-39*
Nevada 51, 52, *52, 54-55*, 57-69, *104*, 105, *105*, 106-07, *108*, 109, *109*, 110
New Helvetia 13
New Mexico 11
Newton, KS 97
Nez Perce Indians 82, 83
Northern Pacific Railroad *95*, 96

O K Corral *115*

GHOST TOWNS

Old Dry Diggings, CA 21. *See also*
   Placerville.
Old Mission Church, Cataldo, ID *46*
Omaha Mine, CA *38-39*
Ophir Mine 52, 60
Oregon Territory 10, 73
Oregon Trail *9*, 10, 89
Oregon Trail, The 10
Osgood, Samuel S. 13
outlaws *81*, 90
Overland Stage Company 80
Overland Trail 25, *28*
Owyhee Basin, ID 82, 83

Parkman, Francis 10, *10*
Parks, Benjamin 9
Perkins, William 29
Peter, T. J. 95
Peterton, KS *94*, 95, *95*, 96
Phoenix, AZ 114
Pierce, E. D. 82
Pikes Peak 69, *69*
Placer County, CA 21
placer mining 48, *48*, 50, 78, 86
Placerville, CA 21, *25*, 25, *27*, *28*,
   40, 42
Plummer, Henry 78, *79*, 80
Polk, James K. 10, 17
Pony Canyon, NV 60, 61
Pony Express 60, 61, 83
Promontory, UT *88-9*
Prudhoe Bay, AK 120

quartz mines 50

railroads *88-9*, 89-101

Rasberry, Bennager 28, 29
Ravine City, CA, 21. *See also*
   Placerville.
Reinhart, Benjamin Franklin 10
religion 46
Reno, NV 51, 105
Rhyolite, NV *108*, 109, *109*, *110*, *124*
"rockers" 48, *49*
Rockies, The 52, 69
Roosevelt, Theodore 109
Roslyn, WA 96
Rough and Ready, CA 33, 34, *35*,
Roughing It 8, 65, 80
Ruby City, ID *81*, 82, 83
Russell, William Green 69

Sacramento Bee 73
Sacramento *Daily Union* 51
Sacramento River 13
St. Louis, Kansas and
   Southwestern Railroad *91*, 100
St. Louis, MO 10, 13, 65
saloons *31*, *43*, *45*, 46, *86*, 97, 100,
   120
San Francisco, CA 10, *12*, 13, 16, 17,
   21, 25, 37, 52, 57
"Sanitary Flour-Sack" affair 65, 68
Santa Fe, NM 89
Santa Fe Railroad 89, 94, 95, 96,
   97, 113
Santa Fe Trail 89, 90, 94
Seward, AK *116-117*
Sheridan, KS 94, 95
Sheridan, Gen. Philip 94
Shoshone Indians 105
Sibley, George 89

Sierra County, CA 21
Sierra Nevada Mountains 21, 51
silver mining *6*, 51, 52, *52*, 57, 59,
   60, 61, 68, 69, 82, 83, 102, 105
Silver City, ID *82*, 82, 83
Silverberg, Robert 37
Sioux Indians 83
Slade, Jack 80, 81, 82
slavery 90, *90*, *91*, 94
"sluices" 48, *49*
Smoky Hill River 94
Sonora, CA 29
Sonora Pass, CA 51
South Dakota 82
South Pass City, WY *83*, 83, *84-85*,
   86
Southern Pacific Railroad 112
stagecoach *73*, *81*
Stimler, Harry 105
Sumner, Edwin Vose *90*
Sutter, John Augustus *13*, 13, 16
Sutter's Mill, CA 8, *14*, 17, 21, 25, 33
Sutter's Fort 16, 17

Taber, William 71
Taylor, Charley 105
Taylor, Zachary 33, 35
Teller, Henry M. 69
Teller House 69, 71
Tiera Coal Mine *111*
Tombstone, AZ 112, *115*
Tonopah, NV *102-3*, *104*, 105, 109
Topeka, KS 95
Topeka State Journal 95
Toqueville, Alexis de 7, 121
Treasure City, NV 68, *68*

Treasure Hill, NV 68
Tritle, Frederick A. 114
Tuolumne County, CA 21
Tuolumne County Museum 29
Twain, Mark 8, 29, 37, 65, 80

Union Pacific Railroad *88-9*
US Dragoons 89
US Sanitary Commission 65

Valdez, AK 121, *122*
Vigilantes of Montana 81
vigilantism *81*, 81, 82, 94
Virginia City, MT 78, *80*, 80, 81, 82
Virginia City, NV *7*, 52, *54-55*, *57*,
   57, *58-59*, *60*, 60, 61, 65
Volcano, CA 25, 28

wagon trains *9*
Wasco, OR *4-5*
Webb, W. F. 94
Webster, Daniel 9
Wells Fargo bank 25, 28
White, Jack 73
White Pine, NV 68
Wichita, KS 97
Wichita Tribune 97
Wilson, Woodrow 112
Wimar, Charles 10
Wittmer, Jacob 17
Woods Crossing, CA 29
Wyoming *1*, 56, 82, 83, 86, 96

Yellowstone 78
Yerba Buena 16
Young, Brigham 16

ACKNOWLEDGMENTS

I am grateful for all the assistance I received while researching and writing
this book. In particular, I would like to thank my editors, Jean Martin and
John Kirk; Joe Warner, who designed the book; Elizabeth Montgomery, who
did the picture research; Florence Norton, who prepared the index; the staffs
of the various historical societies and boards of tourism in the states I have
covered; and my wife, Virginia, who gave me invaluable quiet time and
constructive criticism.

   Among the many printed sources I relied on, the following were especially
useful:

Robert Silverberg, *Ghost Towns of the American West.*
Daniel Fitzgerald, *Ghost Towns of Kansas: A Traveler's Guide.*
Jean Davis, ed. *Shallow Diggin's: Tales From Montana's Ghost Towns.*
Robert L. Brown, *Colorado Ghost Towns, Past and Present*
Ruth E. DeJauregui, *Ghost Towns.*
William S. Greever, *The Bonanza West: The Story of the Western Mining
   Rushes, 1848-1900.*
Samuel Yellen, *American Labor Struggles.*
Rodman Paul, *The Far West And The Great Plains in Transition: 1859-1900.*

PICTURE CREDITS

All pictures courtesy of The Bettmann Archive except the following:
AGS: 76-77
Arizona Office of Tourism: 115 bottom

Brompton Picture Library: 9; 54-55
California State Library, California Section Photograph Collection: 8; 14; 16;
   16; 24 top; 25 top; 29; 30 top; 32 top; 33 bottom; 34 both; 35; 38-39; 41
   both; 45 top; 50 bottom; 52 bottom; 53; 60 bottom; 73
Corcoran Gallery of Art: 10 top
Denver Public Library: 37; 44; 45 bottom; 46 bottom; 47 both; 56 top; 70 top; 71
Larry Friedman, DVM: 1; 2-3
Stuart M. Green: 72
Kansas State Historical Society: 86 top; 90 top; 91 both; 92-93; 94; 95 bottom;
   96 all
Library of Congress: 56 bottom; 90; 101 bottom
Montana Historical Society, Helena: 78; 80 all; 81 bottom; 82 both
National Archives: 87
Nevada Historical Society: 52 top; 62-63; 64; 66-67 both; 68; 104 both; 106-107
New England Stock Photo: © 1989 Roger Bickel 10 bottom; David
   Blankenship 74-75
New York Public Library: 12 bottom
Seaver Center for Western History Research, National History Museum of Los
   Angeles County: 24 bottom; 26-27; 40 bottom; 65; 108 top; 109; 111
© W. Thomas Tizard: 115
UPI/Bettmann: 6; 61; 70 bottom; 86 top; 105; 112; 113; 122-123
US Department of Agriculture: 18-19
University of Michigan Museum of Art: 11 top